ADVENTURES IN
MARINE BIOLOGY

ADVENTURES IN MARINE BIOLOGY

A Tribute to

Old Providence Island

Sid Anderson

Library of Congress Control Number:		2006906726
ISBN 10:	Hardcover	1-4257-2646-1
	Softcover	1-4257-2645-3
ISBN 13:	Hardcover	978-1-4257-2646-1
	Softcover	978-1-4257-2645-4

To order additional copies of this book, contact:
Xlibris Corporation
1-888-795-4274
www.Xlibris.com
Orders@Xlibris.com
24530

CONTENTS

Dedication

To my wife Ali and the leagues of snorkeling adventures we shared at Old Providence Island.

To our daughter Bryn, who went to Providence at age one without choice, and had many of her happiest days there.

To our son Craig, who started his life at Providence snorkeling with his mother, before he was even born! (see photo).

To my daughter Judy, who went with me at age 10 on the first Bahama Adventure in Marine Biology in 1960 (see photo with Dr. Eugene Clark.)

BIRTH OF AN ISLAND

Many millions of years ago, before the appearance of modern man on this beautiful ocean-covered Blue-Green Planet, possibly one night when the stars were brilliant, there came a thundering volcanic eruption on the tropic sea floor. Molten rock roared upwards, causing the ocean to boil, bursting from the sea in cataclysmic fire and smoke. At dawn, catching the sun's first rays, was a new little island of volcanic rock, smoking and steaming, later to be called . . . Providence!

Erupting at the southern end of a probably already existing atoll about 15 miles long, one hill dramatically split. A peak soared to over 1200 feet. One huge rock, barely emerging from the sea, cooled in the form of a gigantic head. To the north, one flow of molten basalt amazingly split into long columns as it cooled—almost like a pile of concrete telephone poles, forming a tiny islet. Several other separate flows of lava barely emerged from the sea, over the centuries to become dramatically beautiful cays, sparkling in the shallow lagoon.

As the lava cooled, egg cells, algae, bacteria, spores, and seeds blew with the wind, were brought by birds, drifted with currents. Most died, but gradually some plants and animals (which were able to survive on bare rock) provided food for the first animals.

Over the centuries dead plants and animals gradually produced soil where larger plants could grow. This precious topsoil, one day to be tilled by farmers, took centuries to develop. Very slowly . . . tropical forests spread over the hills.

Even more slowly, beginning at least 30,000 years ago*, coral reefs grew, especially on the east side where northeast trade winds churned the blue-green shallows into foam and spray, filled with oxygen, just what the coral polyps needed. Creatures more beautiful than an artist could imagine—fish, lobster, sea fans, corals, shells—found new homes here. Land turtles (someday to be called "Ikiti"), boa, iguana, lizzards, and insects arrived on logs—changing slightly over thousands of years, some becoming indigenous species, unique to the island. Ironwood, fruit trees of many kinds, tall grasses near the peak, cockspur, and, by the shore, shallow mangrove swamps—a perfect nursery for baby fish. The new island was now green, and full of LIFE.

During ancient ice-ages, when more of the ocean was frozen, making sea level lower, the island's small streams had formed channels now under the sea—one flowing out to the SE making a pass through the reef, another to the NW forming a channel across the shallows, one day to be called "Channel Mouth" by divers.

Parrot fish fed on the coral, leaving behind brilliant white sand, some of which washed up to form crescent beaches. In the shallows, beds of turtle grass began to grow. Coconuts washed in, sprouted and took root.

When, at last, adventurous people came, in their dugout canoes and sailing ships, they found . . . a paradise!

The first discoverers were probably the Mosquito Indians who came for turtle, fruit, fish. They had their own name for the island, probably forgotten in their ancient oral traditions.

No one knows who were the first European discoverers. Columbus on his later voyages? Balboa in 1513 as he headed for the isthmus to "discover" the Pacific Ocean?

During the 1500's there were undoubtedly many ships which passed within sight, some to wreck on the nearly invisible atolls of Roncador, Quito Suena, Seranilla, Seranna . . . and point-of-reef at Providence.

One survivor, Maese Joan, "the Spanish Crusoe", lived to tell of his eight-year escape from death . . . naked, on strips of sand, eating

---

*   Jorn Geister, Isla de Providencia, FACIES, 1992

turtle and bird's eggs in season, finally catching a few seals. Building a fire tower of driftwood he eventually made smoke signals seen by a passing ship.

Sadly, the Caribbean Monk Seal (Monachus tropicalis) which saved his life, finally providing food and clothing, is now extinct, the last confirmed sighting at Seranilla Bank in 1952. Columbus killed eight in 1494, twentieth century hunters often slaughtered a hundred in a night . . . another beautiful creature, gone from our planet forever.

Providence seems to appear (unnamed) on the beautiful c. 1565 chart of the Caribbean. The oldest known map of the island itself is of 1675, after the Puritans had come and gone. It was called Santa Catalina and shows two churches high atop present day Catalina, possibly built by the Puritans (if they even existed).

It is most likely that the Puritans first named it . . . Providence Island! It's existence had been known by the English at least since 1629 when Robert Rich, Earl of Warwick, during his extensive voyages around the Caribbean, had noted in his diary the "news of an island discovered in the western ocean." As one of the organizers of the Providence company it is likely that he and his crew recommended it as the site for the new colony. When the settlers arrived in 1630 they found a few Dutch already on the island, who became a friendly part of their colony, some working as carpenters.

It is certain that in the earlier years since Columbus many European ships had seen the island in the distance. Some may have wrecked, some landed, even made it their home and given it a long forgotten name. These early "unknown adventurers" left no record, but were fortunate to be the first Providence islanders!

Two other islands have burst from the sea in recent history, Surtsey near Iceland, Anak Krakatau in Indonesia (more similar to Providence, as it is tropical). To read of how life slowly established itself there, see KRAKATAU, by Ian Thornton, Harvard University Press, 1996.

Another book called KRAKATAU, by Simon Winchester, 2002, is the story of the gigantic eruption, tidal waves, destruction over thousands of miles, death of 36,000 people.

Photo of Anak Krakatau, courtesy Volcanological Survey of Indonesia, Bandung. For more photos and information, Google:

Krakatau; also, Birth of an Island, for other new islands in recent history. Occasional earthquakes and eruptions continued through the centuries, and will occur into the future. On Dec. 1, 1999 a magnitude 6.2 earthquake was measured in the western Caribbean.

INTRODUCTION

Come with me! . . . on a blue sky, white cloud morning, when sparkling sunlight, shimmering spray, and salty foam all seem to merge, embracing us as gently as a lover's touch, while we glide "beneath the surface" into the world of coral reefs . . . amid beauty infinitely beyond the creativity of any earthly artist!

Nowhere else on our wonderful Blue-Green Planet can we so effortlessly and quickly enter the world of Nature, much as it was thousands of years ago, seemingly untouched by man. Suddenly, the Sea is our second home. We are friends of the dolphin.

I am not a professional marine biologist, do not have a PhD. I like to call myself an "amateur naturalist", and I would like to invite you to be one also. One can be an amateur naturalist, every hour of every day, right along with whatever else you are doing. It will enrich your life with never ending wonder, growing insight, and hourly excitement and pleasure. I will speak of this again in the final chapter.

On the lighter side, oceanography and marine biology, are emotionally appealing to many young people, with dreams of tropical islands, sailing ships, warm seabreeze in your hair, handsome and beautiful natives dancing under the cocnut palms . . . winking at you . . . easily forgetting the long afternoon chemistry and biology labs, endless reading, many papers to write . . . but, once again, no matter what your profession, you can always be an amateur naturalist.

I have been a grade school and junior high science teacher, have had the great pleasure of knowing dozens of marine biologists and never stop learning from them. Some are among my best friends. I have spent several thousand hours snorkeling and scuba diving, from China to Mexico, the Bahamas to nearly every island of the Caribbean. My wife, Ali, and I have snorkeled with wild dolphins in the Bahamas and Pacific. The sea is our second home.

I hope this small book of shared adventures will take you far from your comfortable armchair, to many of your own "adventures in marine biology".

And, if you haven't been there already, I hope you too will soon experience the shimmering sparkling reefs . . . of Old Providence Island. In 2000, along with the surrounding islands and banks, it became the UNESCO Seaflower Biosphere Reserve, without any doubt the most beutiful area in the Caribbean. Google: Ethnic and biological diversity within the seaflower biosphere reserve, by Marion W. Howard Ph.D., Valeria Pizzaro Ph.D., and June Marie Mow Ph.D.

ADVENTURES AT GARDEN CITY

In 1956, when I was a junior highschool science teacher in Garden City, NY—being inexperienced in consistent discipline—I had a rough time, especially with three brassy boys who had driven a previous teacher to resign. On the first day a boy came up to warn me: "Mr. Anderson, I hope you are a strict teacher. This class has been together a long time—they are tough." But, sadly, teaching previously in a wonderful private school, I was not yet experienced in discipline. As class started, Dave Conway (14-yr-old eighth grader) was sitting in the back row grinning, wearing my jacket which he had taken from the closet. I didn't know what to do.

All my life I had been in love with Biology and Nature. I spent hours each night preparing. I really wanted to help these kids catch the excitement of the wonders of Nature. I showed them live amoeba moving in search of food, to engulf it, then dividing into two new creatures. We marveled at Euglena, a singled celled swimming organism which also has chlorophyll. It has characteristics of both plant and animal! Scientists had to create a new kingdom, Protista.

I tried to help them be amazed at the very existence of the Universe, of LIFE. My students called me "Mr. Amoeba". But, in my enthusiasm to teach, when they would get a bit unruly, instead of calmly restoring order, I would flare up angrily. It took them by surprise . . . I was inconsistent.

I loved the seventh graders, bright eyes looking up at me, full of questions, not yet sophisticated. But, sadly, problems continued in eighth grade. I could have stuck it out, but, as midyear approached, I had become quite sure I did not want to continue as a public school teacher. The assistant principal would stand at the window, later asking me why I let the students talk so freely. It was very painful for me. I handed in a resignation letter. I was heart-warmed when all the students signed a petition asking me to stay . . . but it was too late. I escaped to a windjammer cruise in the Bahamas, to skindive and try to pay expenses collecting Queen Helmet Shells.* I had taken a scuba course the year before and won two spearfishing contests with our club.

We flew from Miami to Bimini just across the Gulf Stream and there was the Polynesia, a gorgeous schooner, anchored just offshore. I couldn't wait to get in that water. Accustomed to 15-foot visibility in Connecticut's Long Island Sound, I wanted to see if it was really true about "crystal-clear" Bahamian waters. I was down the gangplank with mask and flippers. The Gulf Stream was flowing northward at a fast clip, so I hung on, amazed at seeing every detail on the bottom 80 feet below. Then I carefully tested to see if I could hold my own against the current. I could, so I dove under the ship, not only seeing bow and stern, but far into the distance (maybe over 200 feet!). Large ocean jacks swam by. It was true. This was what I had dreamed of!

Right in Nassau harbor I found big Helmet shells. (Later, with more experience, my thoughts changed about collecting shells commercially. Better to enjoy them in Nature. Too much collecting can lead to scarcity, even extinction.) We went from island to island, wonderful sailing, beautiful diving.

I remember one night sailing across the Bahama Passage, I had a turn at the wheel. As ships bore down on us and passed, under the brilliant stars, healing over a bit, our schooner surged forward through the spray. I was "captain of a clipper ship, sailing to the orient!"

During those days I had a brainstorm . . . which changed my life! I would organize "Adventures in Marine Biology", a diving-learning vacation-expedition, inviting a marine biologist to join us, giving us two classes a day, and we would help in his or her research project. I was excited! (So far as I know I was the first to offer a learning-vacation with accompanying expert. Today you see dozens of advertisements in many magazines.)

I sent a story to SKIN DIVER MAGAZINE, placed a small advertisement. My friend Paul Tzimoulis, editor-publisher, printed my story in the July 1959 edition. Applications came. My plan to charter the Polynesia fell through, but I found the Bahama Queen, 110-foot single-engined ship. Owner would install a diving ramp on stern, provide space for a compressor (which I soon rented in Miami, to be delivered to the ship along with 12 brand new scuba tanks). I had little money, never planned to make a profit. This was for fun and learning—an adventure!

Marine biologist, Dr. Victor Springer would make a collection of Bahamian reef fish, using rotenone (a non-poisonous chemical which blocks oxygen intake). We would collect with small nets.

I placed a tiny classified for a cook, to show up at the Miami dock. I made check-lists, imagining each day hour-by-hour. We would follow a strict buddy-system, wear inflatable life jackets. When some complained, I asked: "If your buddy got into trouble, 300 yards from the boat in rough water, could you bring him in?" There were no more complaints.

I studied the charts, talked with Bahamian divers, studied YACHTSMAN'S GUIDE TO BAHAMAS. I even got a free trip to Florida by driving someone's car. Delivering the car, taking a taxi to the dock, there was the BAHAMA QUEEN, looking HUGE, impressive! About 25 men were sitting everywhere, waiting for someone? who? They were applicants for ships's cook, waiting for ME! Now what was I going to do? I couldn't interview them all! Luckily, my problem was quickly solved. Leo came up to me: "Don't try to talk with all those cooks—I'm your man. I've had experience on ships, will plan your menus, do the shopping, make your divers well-fed and happy." His aggressive self-assurance won me immediately. He specified that he would not wash dishes. Short of money, I would do it. Leo was off to his cabin to make menus and shopping list.

Compressor and scuba tanks arrived on a lift-truck, were hoisted into place. To test it, we filled a tank, the owner teaching me details of operation. The new dive-ramp seemed OK. I explored the ship, putting diver's names on each cabin.

Leo took me to a wholesale supermarket, catering especially to ships. We soon filled eight shopping carts! Luckily the manager, let me pay 25%, balance on return (when I would have final payments from members). We bought crates of beer and soda, which divers could buy (a serious mistake, as the crew did away with most of it!) Hiring a van, we were soon back at the ship, loading everything into the galley. Divers were arriving. We would sail in early evening.

Docked far up a river in the heart of Miami, the winding trip down river in the sunset was spectacular, across the bay, out into the Gulf Stream (a bit rough), we were at sea. Before dawn we anchored at our first dive spot, south of Bimini, Bahamas!

Shallow calm waters, lobsters under ledges, sting rays, a nurse shark, Bimini was a good first dive. A spectacular Spotted Eagle Ray rippled slowly past, as cameras clicked. Everyone was content. It was a good opportunity for me to see how everyone handled themselves. We had our first meals. Leo was as great as he predicted. Our first two seminars had us looking forward to the coming days.

Before sunset we were on our way toward Nassau, this time across the shallow bank north of Andros, no coral, nothing but sand, most of us lying on the deck, heads over the side, watching unending thousands of huge red and orange starfish passing below us. Mesmerized, we finally wandered off to bed, except for me. I had to wash a mountain of dishes! (I should have hired a boy in Bimini—too late) Then I must refill twelve scuba tanks. Luckily, against the throb of the engine, the compressor was fairly quiet.

At Andros we anchored in calm waters inside a little island. Some of us were spear fishing at the edge of the open sea. My buddy and I had each speared a fish when we saw a shark coming rapidly straight for us. Wisely, we dropped the fish, just in time. The shark realized we weren't fish, turned abruptly and grabbed a fish on the bottom. At the same moment two large Cobia (aggressive predatory fish about four feet long) swam in and took the other fish, violently tearing it to pieces! This was the first of many experiences, and accounts read, which convinced me that sharks and other predators can detect the vibrations of a wounded fish more quickly and from much further away than the smell of blood.

Returning towards the boat, what do we see but Eugenie Clark (who can be a bit macho, like us all!) snorkeling with her two daughters and my daughter Judy, with a fish on her spear. I doubt that she realized at that time that she was setting herself up as shark bait—not to speak of the girls!

A few miles before Nassau we stopped at a dramatic reef where "20,000 Leagues Under the Sea" was filmed. It was here that I found two giant Loggerhead turtles which all of us had fun riding. The first was lying on the bottom, apparently asleep, under a coral head. As I swam back to the boat to tell the others, I saw another. We soon caught them both, quickly learning that the best way to hold them is fore and aft, one hand behind its neck and the other over its tail. This way it can't scratch you with its flippers, and you can pull its head up when you want it to swim you to the surface, or let it down for a ride. We took turns riding them for an hour, then it was lunchtime so we put them in our fiberglass dingy while we ate. After lunch we found they had been eating also—big bites out of the fiberglass! So watch out for those jaws if you catch a big turtle.

After lunch we rode them again, some snorkeling, Dr. Eugenie Clark with scuba, while Stan Waterman took movies (see photo). It was a memorable day!

On our way east from Nassau to Abaco we passed a pod of Pilot Whales. They may have been False Killer Whales which are so similar I would not have the expertise to know. About twenty of them swam slowly past us, and I had the urge to circle back and swim with them. But in those days no one had swum with whales, so we were overly cautious.

In 2001 in Puerto Escondido, on Pacific coast of Mexico, I swam with a whale. We saw it about half mile away cruising slowly on the surface, maybe a Gray Whale feeding. When it turned towards us we stopped the boat, watching. When it was 100 yards away and still coming, I jumped in and immediately heard its radar-like sounds and then felt it "drumming" on my chest, like finger tips tapping! Visibility was poor, so I didn't see it till it passed ten feet under me.

It then approached the boat, raised its head and looked at Omar and Carlos. They saw its eye for several seconds. Then it raised its tail, and dove. I wish I could have communicated my friendship!

The charter boat had the advantage of mobility, but the Bahamas are usually windy. Then we had a minor wreck! We ran onto coral in middle of the night, our captain not reading the chart carefully enough to know that tides run on and off the banks, so we were moving sideways with the tide as we went north along coast of Abaco . . . till we hit, damaging the propeller. While repairs were made, we explored the wreck of the Adirondack which had gone onto the reefs during Civil War . . . for exactly the same reason.

WE DISCOVER OLD PROVIDENCE

So I started looking for an island with calm waters, offering safe diving no matter what the wind. After poring over hundreds of charts . . . I found Old Providence island! . . . the only true atoll in the Caribbean, a beautiful mountainous island, miles of reefs one could explore for several lifetimes. I started writing letters, reading guide books. Almost no tourists had been there, no scuba divers. The English speaking islanders had no hotels, no airstrip. How could we make contact? Then through Dr. James Parsons we found Marco Archbold who had translated his book, an islander just an hour away in New York City. He visited, taught us everything. We were on our way to Old Providence Island!

HOW OCEAN RACING CHANGED THE LIVES OF PROVIDENCE FISHERMEN

It was very early Monday morning Jan. 16, 1967 when Alfredo Carrera (island student on vacation) and I loaded the 14-ft aluminum runabout for the long trip to Point-of-Reef, out of sight on the northeastern horizon, seeking the 1963 wreck of the MORNING STAR, steel-hulled ocean racer (YACHTING, Aug. 1963).

Islanders make this ten-mile trip daily in sailing catboats, but for us it would be a voyage not without danger. If we capsized we could not recover like a catboat, so we prepared carefully. We took two outboards, extra five gallons of gas, food and water, snorkeling gear and spear guns. In a large plastic bucket with clamp-on lid I had my 35mm camera, underwater Nikonos, flash light, first aid kit, compass, 200 feet of extra anchor line, spare anchor, fishing gear, knife, and lunch.

The weather, though bright and clear, was blustery, but I had already waited two weeks and the NE trade winds seldom drop below 10 mph in January, so we left the beach at 7:45 AM and headed east out of Catalina harbor, past the wreck of James Rankin's REMBREAU (once a proud island schooner), across the shallow bar, and immediately were bucking choppy whitecaps of considerable size for inside the reef. We continued due east toward the reef but the gusty wind was obviously rising. Drenched with stinging spray, we found it painful to look into the wind, making slow progress. Even at half speed the bow would occasionally dig under and the propeller often broke surface with a roar.

On an average morning at least twenty island fishermen would be out by this time, but we saw only two about half a mile ahead of us, their flour-sack sails white against the green-blue of the inner reefs. I would guess in those years there were about 100 cat boats, most with sails actually made of flour sacks (the manufacturer's names clearly printed), the others?—cut from the sails of the MORNING STAR!

As we approached the reef the chop and surge smoothed out, but it was still difficult to see the hundreds of coral heads inside the reef. Providence had miles and miles of them, coming to within inches of the surface. Alfredo was in the bow, directing me with a raised hand on our weaving course. Occasionally I would have to cut the motor until we drifted off a swallow reef.

Gradually we turned northeast, running parallel to the reef, the boom of the ocean rollers thundering onto the reef close on our right. Beyond the reef to the east was open ocean for 1000 miles, Panama 200 miles to the south, Jamaica 350 to the northeast, Mosquito coast of Nicaragua 100 miles to the west. Within 50 miles were three of the most dangerous coral banks in the Western Hemisphere, uninhabited—Roncador, Quito Suena, Serranilla—having only unmanned lights. Providence itself has only one lighthouse, low on a southeast hill, often obstructed by trees on east and west!—not visible at all from the north.

No wonder there are so many wrecks at Point of Reef! Ships coming down from the north see the beautiful island far in the distance—then, without warning and too late to turn, breakers just ahead, they wreck on the reef. Even the Jacksonian, participating in the 1835 British survey, wrecked there.

Squinting through the blur of stinging salt, drenched and shivering, my right arm already aching from wrestling with the motor—I was thinking of the MORNING STAR, not coming from the north, like so many that wrecked, but from Panama to the south.

Fooled by the notoriously changing currents, closed in by poor visibility, she was not to the west of Providence as planned, but to the east. Shortly after midnight, under auxiliary power and sail, she was suddenly in shoal water, giant combers dead ahead. Before there was time to make any decision—she was on the reef, striking again and again, then healing far over high on the coral, breakers thundering across the deck. The five on board were swept into the shallows, but managed to get back aboard to launch the dingy. Even in my imagination I found myself tensing every muscle, my jaw set. Alfredo looked back at me quizzically, "What's up?" "Just thinking about the MORNING STAR" I said. We laughed, but not in fun.

We talked about whether or not we could make it today. I was doubtful. Three hours had passed and I wondered if we had made four miles, at least six to go. We were tired and cold, so we decided to stop and spear fish for awhile.

We were soon in the pleasant 78 degree water, warmer than the air that day! It was a fabulous reef, seldom visited by island divers. We soon had six lobsters (langusta) and a few fish. A shark circled. By the time I got my camera—it was gone, but I got a good shot of Alfredo with lobster (see photo). Hungry, we climbed aboard to munch sandwiches and oranges.

If anything, the wind was up, but the sun was beautiful, and we saw a sail at least a mile north. "Let's go for it!" So again we headed north along the thundering reef snaking through the coral heads. Less than an hour passed when Alfredo suddenly pointed and grinned, "the MORNING STAR!" It took me a moment to spot it, just one persistent dark bump on the horizon which didn't move as the breakers did. It grew rapidly. Soon we could see the curve of the deck facing us with bow to northwest. Amazingly we were able to motor right up through the shallows in her lee to anchor within 50 feet and wade over a knee-deep coral ledge, to climb aboard! Peaks of Providence were dimly visible a long ten miles south.

It was a wild scene, and we didn't try to talk above the thunder of the surf. Breakers extended to the horizon to the south, and a half mile to the west. We felt very unprotected!

I took two rolls of Ektachrome photos from the boat, and then Kodachrome with the waterproof Nikonos as we waded through the surf, the first photos that I know of since the wreck.

All movable objects had already been taken. Later even the lead keel would be salvaged. So, without even a brass fitting to remember her by, we started back, this time at exhilarating speed, wet as ever, Alfredo doing masterful navigating. In deeper water Alfredo landed two Barracuda trolling before we rounded Morgan's Head, and stepped out on the beach in town at 2:20.

For weeks I tried to meet Sammy Taylor who found the crew of the Morning Star in their dingy, and towed them back to the island. Without him, they could easily have had a second wreck on a coral head—and not survived. Mr. Ray (Victor Howard) helped the crew during their five days on the island, staying at Winston's. The captain, whose feet were badly cut on the coral, needed two men to help him get to the dispensary.

Crew members later wrote Mr. Ray offering to buy the wheel and pay for shipment. It was a beauty, about three feet and brass bound. He had it recovered, packed, and shipped off to Miami.

Today I found photos of Alfredo trolling past Morgan Head, and wrote him a letter in care of his school in San Andres. He would be in his seventies now. I hope he will answer!

(I later corresponded with Bryan McDermott, crewman, sending him 19 photos. He sent me the four-page report of loss, written in Providence June 30, 1963, by Fuller E. Callaway III, owner.)

TRIBUTE TO CAPTAIN ULRIC

In 1965, when we went to Providence for the first time with our year-old daughter, Bryn, there was only one way to go—deck passage, from Colon, Panama, with captain Ulric Archbold on his Motor Vessel ARCABRA. Occasionally, other small ships came and went (the Cisne, Victoria, Gloria, Laguna, Wave Crest, Rosa Eugenia, Janet), but only captain Ulric sailed a fairly regular schedule, about every 10-12 days.

James Rankin's ships had sunk the schooner "Rembreau" right in the harbor in front of his house. There were no passenger ships, or planes. The ARCABRA was the only way—to the hospital, home on vacation, off to seek a job, or for adventurous wanderers like us. Captain Ulric knew that Old Providence Island depended on him. He cared.

The seas can be extremely rough between San Andres and Providence. He once had to turn back when within thirty miles, the wind screaming right out of the north. He couldn't make it. In Jan. 1967, the Rosa Eugenia had to turn back, barely making it the next night. But the Wave Crest that same week almost sank and had to turn back.

The ARCABRA had no cabins, only two bunks (for captain and mate). As Ali was nursing Bryn, the mate kindly let us use his bunk, way up forward, starboard of the bridge. As long as there was room for one more, passengers crowded onto the covered main deck, squeezing in between crates, 55-gal-drums of gasoline for the island's handful of cars and motors, bags of rice, packages from relatives, furniture, saddles, bolts of cloth, a sewing machine, mail sack (personally escorted by Mr. Carol Robinson, island postman)—everything islanders desperately needed. On return trip: cattle, oranges, pigs, chickens, iguanas, frozen fish and lobsters, empty drums, Carol with another mail sack (he hated his job, because he got seasick), and a new group of deck passengers.

Leaving Colon, through the breakwater, suddenly it was the open ocean. As the first waves hit us, a drum broke loose, crashing over the railing into the sea. There were grim faces, no words or laughter. The ARCABRA offered no comfort, very real danger—single engine, drums of gasoline on deck. Between Colon and San Andres Island, the NE trade winds sweep across 800 miles of open Caribbean Sea. No wonder it is usually rough. Twelve years later island families were devastated when a ship carrying students—went down. Our very special friends, Carol & Eloisa Robinson, lost two sons.

Arriving at San Andres, low hills and coconut groves covering most of the seahorse-shaped island, we had a few hours ashore before continuing the last forty miles to Providence. A huge dredge was pumping sand ashore, to improve the beach while deepening the harbor, bringing up million-year-old fossil coral and shells—the first we had ever seen, helping to stretch our minds beyond clocks and calendars.

Leaving Ali sitting on some rocks with Bryn, I, the "macho husband", walked down the beach to get a closer look at a fascinating sailing ship anchored north of the ARCABRA. Not knowing that Bryn had fallen and knocked out a tooth, I strolled slowly back. Too far away to call, Ali and Bryn suffered alone. So, sadly and in pain, without even a swim, we went back on board for the final long night to Providence. We wondered how many people before us had made the crossing on that fragrant mattress.

On future trips I remember spending hours on the bridge, listening, as captain Ulric shared experiences of the sea and his island. One night, the phosphorescence was brilliant. Luminous shapes, around the bow, appeared, and then were gone. Some were basket ball size, others elongated. They were not dolphins. We never knew. It remained a dramatic mystery.

It was about 2AM when we were suddenly in calm water, in the lee of the island. I left Ali and Bryn in the narrow bunk, climbed a wooden ladder, out onto the open top deck. There was a quiet voice beside me, captain Ulric's son, Lloyd: "There she is, Mr. Sid, Old Providence, our rocky little island." It was an emotional moment for me—after a year of saving and planning, we were here!

The island was dark, not a single light, hills dimly silhouetted against the stars. Having studied the chart, I knew there were patch reefs on this west side and marveled that captain Ulric could approach at night. Obviously he knew it all by heart, keeping close to shore in two-to-three fathoms.

Now there were headlights coming around a hill, flashing up and down on an obviously very rough road, going north parallel to us towards town. "It's the pickup truck coming to meet us." We learned later that this pickup with wood benches was the island's only "bus" or "taxi". It was always ready, to take the nurse to birth a baby, or a sick person to the only doctor.

A few lights came into view as we entered the harbor, anchoring till dawn. Most of the passengers went ashore in small boats, and home by foot or pickup, or boat to Catalina (a small separate island north of the harbor.) We didn't yet have a place to stay, but hoped it would be on the east side where captain Ulrich would go come daylight, so we stayed on board, talking briefly with Bob Marx who came down to meet us.

When unloading was finished in mid-morning the ARCABRA started back south, around SW Bay and past the lighthouse, then north inside the barrier reef, to finally anchor at Smoothwater Bay in front of captain Ulric's home.

He had HAM radio friends around the world, spending many hours at this favorite hobby. But now there would be barely a day of rest. Islanders were already packing for his next trip, driving livestock to town, catboats full of oranges, boys catching iguanas to send to San Andres, maybe a young person deciding to seek his fortune in California, someone's mother (too ill to be treated by Dr. Conolly and Miss Bress, the nurse) off to the hospital. She would be given a bunk. For the rest, once again, there would be a spot somewhere on the deck.

Suddenly a bull is led running towards the dock. Children scatter, screaming and laughing. Adults dodge behind empty gasoline drums waiting to be loaded. Long poles are lashed across foredeck, horns of cattle lashed to these. Before leaving dock, cattle are sucured in a sling, faced towards water and given a sudden twist of their tail—they bolt into the sea! Lashed alongside a canoe they are swum out to Arcabra and hoisted aboard, total of 15 and 70 passengers. Once there were 140! No one looks forward to this night voyage. With nothing in the hold, cargo and passengers riding high, it will be violent tossing and rolling to San Andres.

On Jan. 20, 1967, Capt. Ulric agreed to tell me his life story. I turn on my tape recorder:

"Well, as far as I know the first Archbold that came here was Capt. Francis Archbold, an Englishman from Scotland, got a grant of land from the Spanish government, don't know how much but the Archbolds inherit 25 acres. He might have had more and give it up to the slaves. Right in this area it was actually called Archbold down toward Bottom House, right on the marine chart of 1833.

He had two sons Francis Jr. and James, my great great grandfather. My grandfather Ephreum had a son, Francis, Mr. Alpheus' father. Quite a few girls, Ammaret, Jepirah, and Ellen. Another son, James, lived in town, was the grandfather of Dr. Connolly's mother. My grandfather, Ephreum, had eight sons, all sea captains but one. My father, James, was the eldest and had a twin brother, Thomas, Litenes, Marshall, Francis, Victor, James, and January (we call him Jamie). Those were the eight sons. Thomas was a school teacher, but he died quite young. Frederick was the first naval captain in the Colombian navy, two ships, auxiliary (sail and motor.) He didn't go very far. He drowned on a trip from Cartagena to San Andres, was missing off the boat. Government had the boat tied up and navy was scrapped, until around 1934, when they got the boat they have now. Continent had no seafaring people at all.

This was a small island, not much doing, so they had to go to sea, mostly turtle fishing. The only cargo was mangos, chickens, pigs, export to Panama, and to Port Limon, and Bocas del Toro. Turtle shell was worth as high as $10 a pound, but after the first world war it dropped suddenly, plastic invented. Recently went back up to $4, most to Japan, Germany. The clear thick shell is worth twice as much as the dark.

Yes, the house where I was born still exists, three houses from here, Mr. Rudolph Newball, another house, then my father's (no one lives there, just close up) next to my cow pen on the road.

There were six of us, three boys and three girls. My mother was from San Andres, her father an English Jew, came out on sailing boat from Jamaica and just stayed, used to work in office with municipal judge. My father was captain on sailing ships, long voyages, did not see much of the old man. He would come for maybe 8 days, then gone for 3-4 months carrying coconut.

I lived right here, went to school, took care of cows. I was the youngest brother, took care of the fish pots, milk the cow, before school. Fish pots were woven of cane and grass, some of wire, very seldom put in bait. Put it where fish school, one goes in, others follow, thinking it a good place to hide (laughing).

First teacher was Julio Gaillardo from San Andres. Later the Baptist mission opened school; teacher was David Allen May of SA, born 1902. Adventists came later; one sister and myself are Adventists.

I made my first trip out from here in 1927 to Barranquilla, building breakwater at Magdellena River mouth, then back home for about three months, then to Colon and join a steamship out of New York, hauling aluminum from British Guiana to New Orleans, sometimes to Wilmington, Delaware. I worked in New York for about three years, painting, had a contracting business with two other fellows. Then father got sick and I came back home. That's when I started into carpentry on my own.

My father died. I was married to my first wife, had Lloyd and a daughter when wife died. Two years after I married this wife, had four daughters, and plenty of grandchildren now, as you can see!

(laughing) Daughter from first wife is a nurse. Most of my children went to high school on the continent, one still in school in Puerto Rico. One lives in Miami, one here, one in hospital.

My older brother and I owned another ship down in Panama called the ANTONIO, used to run from Colon to Bocas del Torro.

He lives in Colon and still makes that run. I sold out to him six years ago and came back here, bought this boat in Cayman Islands.

(I asked if there was any truth in the story that he studied navigation by peeking through cracks in the wall?)

Well, yes. The old man didn't like me to go out to sea. He spent enough of his life at sea, just like now, most captains never want their sons to go to sea, easier to do something ashore. But he taught my brother navigation. I was just a little kid at the time and tried to peek around to see what they were doing. Sort of in the blood . . . I did pick up a little from him, then on the steamship I started learning navigation, didn't plan to use it, but started back to sea after my stretch at carpentry, during the last war we become isolated here. Nothing could come in from anywhere, a lot of submarines around, and everybody scared to go out. So Dr. Connolly volunteer and take a boat out to Cartegena so we could buy some foodstuff.

The ARCABRA I bought in 1960. During the war I was on a sailing schooner called the MARY B (V?), then the BOGOTA, used to run between Barranquilla and Buena Ventura (?). Quite a few small ships used to run from Santa Marta with bananas.

Since that time, as you see, I have been slaving (laughing) more or less, for the people of Providence. It's not a profitable business coming in here, but it has sort of become a responsibility more or less, I guess. (I asked . . . future of Providence?)

Well, to be frank with you, I would not like to see this place become very commercialized, Most people from outside would be coming to make money and go back out. I would like to see somebody come here, stay here, and live here. I actually suggest we never let this island be commercialized. With a small airport, permanent connections with San Andres, where people can come for a quiet weekend, call it a rest island. Big hotel business would attract gambling. Island population is small yet, much people migrate from here. I've got six daughters, and the six of them are in the United States! (laugh)

With the setting of the island, best to keep it as it is, just a better communication, light and electrical power . . . but a commercial island, I hope it never comes to that. The island is healthful. I don't think anybody would ever starve here. You could always find something to eat before sun go down. (laugh)

Take San Andres, for instance. All the business was people from outside, many Europeans, make money and send it out. Islanders are not better off than before it was a free port.

(airport?) I will be the happiest man the day I see a plane pitch here. People who can't afford plane will be plenty for me.

(discussed navigation into harbor at Providence, a fitting way to close our memories of Captain Ulric)

Course from San Andres is about N 10 degrees E. Then, off Lazy Hill (we call this Signal Hill, you come down here till you open that hill. One hill is lapping the other. Come down till you get them apart, they open like that. As soon as they open, you make a sharp turn and steer right for that opening, steer NE. After you get here you can follow the land, just about 50 yards out, that's where you get the deepest water, out there is shallow. That is a bar out here. Come right down till you open SCISSORS HILL. This is the safest channel." We sat quietly for awhile.

Captain Ulric Archbold has made his last voyage, his final HAM radio conversation . . . On behalf of all friends of Old Providence Island, I want to say: . . . We will remember you always, with our very deepest gratitude . . . Thank you, Captain Ulric!

PURITAN PRIVATEERS OF PROVIDENCE ISLAND

Only two years after the Mayflower sailed to the New World in 1620, the Seaflower carried another group of Puritans, not to Massachusetts, but to a tiny island in the western Caribbean. They were backed by the Providence Company (powerful and wealthy aristocrats), so they named it "Providence Island", escaping religious conflicts to commit themselves to freedom in the New World and, hopefully, to make a profit. What courage!

One of their organizers, Robert Rich, Earl of Warwick, a longtime explorer of the Caribbean, had learned of this apparently uninhabited island, a perfect place for their planned new colony. However, on many early charts, It appears as Santa Catalina, even on one of 1675, after the colony was gone.

Even many modern maps don't show it, but the best ones do. Drawing an imaginary line from Florida to Panama, about 110 miles off the coast of Nicaragua (uninhabited reefs to the north and an unbroken 800 miles of Caribbean Sea to the east), probably the most dangerous area in the new world to navigate . . . if you look carefully, you will see two tiny islands. The larger is San Andres, and, 40 miles to the north is the most beautiful—mountainous, reef-encircled— Providence Island. Today it is usually called Isla de Providencia or Old Providence Island, to distinguish it from New Providence Island, Bahamas, and Prvidencialis in the Turks & Caicos.

Some of the North American colonists (in Virginia, Bermuda, Connecticut, Massachusetts, Maine, and their backers in England) had thought of these early settlements as just a first step towards major English colonies in Central America. The Puritans of Providence Island were aware of this.

Amazingly, on this mountainous, thorny and forested volcanic island, they decided to grow cotton! Wild remnants still exist today. But it was hard, hard work! Even if you walked the island today, with most of the forest now gone, you might think it impossible.

From the beginning they had problems. Farmers were required to give half of their produce to the company, and many hours of labor in building five forts with 14 cannon. They had no vote in island affairs. They were concerned that they might even lose their land in the future, after having put so much labor in clearing and planting. Soldiers did not all share the religious convictions of the other colonists. It seems they had far more internal strife than the New England Puritans. Common "crimes" were "swearing, drunkenness, sabbath-breaking".

Also colonists were increasingly aware that their leaders were engaging in a growing lucrative trade with the Mosquito Indians on the nearby coast, had sent the king's son to be educated for three years in England.

So because life was so difficult, and even though their planners in England condemned slavery, in the New World their Puritan beliefs allowed them . . . to acquire slaves! Some Pequot Indian slaves were sent from New England and hundreds of Africans were bought at Caribbean slave markets. When Pimienta ended the colony in 1641 he captured 350 English and 381 slaves (who he sold in Cartagena.) He learned that earlier there had been even more, but the Puritans reduced the number, fearing a possible uprising. They had sent many to St. Kitts and Bermuda, and had actually killed fifty "for conspiracy." These tragic realities of the Puritan colony are revealed in the extensively researched 1993 book by Karen Ordahl Kupperman, PROVIDENCE ISLAND 1630-1641, The Other Puritan Colony.

Struggling with these difficulties (even in a "tropical paradise") they often saw Spanish ships passing—bringing fantasies of acquiring wealth more easily than by farming—finally, they yielded to the temptation, were granted "letters of privateering" from their founding company in England—and became the "Puritan privateers of Providence Island". With highly fortified Providence as their base, they spread to Saint Andrews Island, Bluefields on the coast, and roved the nearby routes of the Spanish galleons . . . with great success.

However, their colony was shortlived. Angered by this harassment, Spain sent a fleet under Pimienta, who, after two failures (in 1635 and 1640) finally (in l641) captured the island (losing one ship on the reef), and deported the Puritans.

The final chapter, little known, came soon after. Those first winters for the Massachusetts Puritans were so dismal that, knowing of their fellow Puritans on a beautiful tropical island, some decided to emigrate—a second time. So they sailed for Providence Island, not knowing they were—too late. Arriving off the harbor they were fired on by the Spanish. They had no choice but to return to Massachusetts, once again forced to learn to survive those frigid winters.

What happened to the defeated Puritan privateers? There is little information, but apparently, allowed by Pimienta to leave, they scattered to the coast, and to many islands, some say Tortuga, or even back to England. Their ambitious colonial dream had failed, but some continued as privateers.

This was a closed chapter in the history of Providence. With a few Dutch and other unknown earlier settlers, and a few Spanish soldiers following the Puritan's defeat, so far as we know not one single Puritan returned to Providence. They did leave houses, forts, cannon, broken bowls, ancient bottles, cotton . . . unknown plants and trees . . . and a name—Providence Island!

I LOVE BIOLOGY

I love Biology . . . because it is the story of the wonders of LIFE. It is about the miracle of Birth, the interdependence of plants and animals, Photosynthesis, growth, the search for food, escape from danger, health and disease, the wonders of Love and sex, fun and

Adventure, competition, success and failure, survival of the fittest, and finally . . . the mystery of Death.

I love Biology . . . because it includes the great Rain Forests of Planet Earth, the Oceans and Coral Reefs.

I love Biology . . . because it includes Old Providence Island!

WE DISCOVER OLD PROVIDENCE ISLAND

It was no accident. We searched the charts of the Caribbean for the most remote, spectacular, untouched, inexpensive coral-reef-island—with calm diving waters every day, in any wind or weather. Asking a lot? Yes . . . we were looking for the very best, the most wonderful island in the Caribbean.

We might have chosen Grand Cayman, but it's flat—or Cozumel, but it had already been discovered by too many. We might have gone to Roatan (another very beautiful island), but we found Old Providence first! One glance at US Oceanographic chart 1370 and we were hooked—craggy volcanic peaks covering the tiny six-mile island, atoll-like barrier reefs surrounding coral-gilded lagoons!

Five years earlier, I had taken groups to the Bahamas on skin-diving learning-vacations, ADVENTURES IN MARINE BIOLOGY. Wind was often a problem. Old Providence looked perfect, protected waters in any weather, so we started looking for someone who had been there. James Parsons, told us about Marco Archbold who had translated his book about the islands, and was now in New York City, only two hours away! Born and bred on Providence, recently returned from designing a new island water system, Marco was eager to meet us. He came to Connecticut several times, his fascinating true stories, turning our wishful thinking into immediate plans—to go!

It was no simple matter, for we were almost penniless—and had a baby! Marco had answers for all our problems: how to get there, where to live cheaply, what to take. We advertised our tiny garage-apartment for six-month sub-let, bought a two-seater inflatable "kayak", arranged to park our old station wagon with diving friend in Miami, made list of basic necessities, saved every possible penny, renewed our passports, bought tickets Miami-to-Panama for November—we were committed!

How could we pay for our trip, now that we had bitten off far more than was "reasonable"? Once I had almost paid for a windjammer cruise in the Bahamas by collecting helmet shells for a seashell dealer* Could we do that? Of course they would not pay in advance, but we wrote the NY Museum of Natural History. Yes, they would love to get a shell collection from such a remote spot, never collected before. We went to NY, goggled at the exhibits, were shown one of the rarest shells in the Caribbean: "Cypraea surinamensis" (Google for color photo and details) . . . they would be most happy to get another! So, we had another daydream—bought a few shell books. We soon learned that surinamensis lived under rocks in deep water, so, without scuba, we were not likely to find it.

We bought a baby-table for Bryn, underwater cameras & film, designed and built a collapsible raft. Every available penny—was spent.

Finally, it was late October, station wagon packed, key passed to young couple sub-letting our apartment. Autumn glory of Connecticut hills was fading as we started driving south—it was Halloween day. Was this "trick", or "treat"? We had never been so excited!

We climbed the Washington Monument, practicing with our movie camera. As inexperienced parents we were terrified when Bryn choked on a bit of chicken cartilage at a South Carolina "redneck" restaurant—but, on impulse, we had her upside-down, gave quick hard pressure on diaphragm—it popped out! The Heimlich maneuver had not yet been named.

Near St. Petersburg, Florida, at sunset, we rented a cabin by the shore. At sunrise we were the only people on the beach. Bryn found our first seashell!

At a highway rest stop, a chance to crawl, Bryn suddenly was up a flight of stairs, grinning gleefully down at us through the wide railing. Should we go up to get her—or stay below to catch her? We did both, and Bryn was safely back in our arms. In Miami, the park grass was so full of prickly burrs she couldn't crawl, so had to settle for the hood of our car.

At John Pennekamp Coral Reef State Park at Key Largo (after starting a lifetime addiction to Key Lime Pie!) we, at last, could snorkel, marveling, eye-to-eye, at a baby ten-inch Barracuda in the shallows. By luck we met a young diver with rented boat (even with a small glass bottom) who invited us to join him in searching for a galleon. He "knew the exact location", so, with no hesitation, we were off. Bryn could safely crawl, looking down at us through the glass while we dove.

He couldn't find the galleon—"it must be within a hundred yards!", but we did find, by chance, one of the most spectacular spots we have ever seen (before or since). On outer edge of the reef, surrounded by dramatic coral heads, a giant grouper was framed in a magnificent coral doorway, moving in and out with the surge. Years later we would have known it was a "cleaning station", but at the time we didn't look carefully enough to see the cleaner fish.* Google: "CLEANING SYMBIOSIS" by Conrad Limbaugh, Scientific American, August, 1961.

After a rest with Bryn, Ali went back in, and there was a shark, a big one, swimming slowly not ten feet away—her first! She thought this was "normal", but when our friend joined her, he didn't think so, was back in the boat in a flash! Ali decided she had better join us too.

It was nearly time to fly. We headed back to Miami, only stopping for one more Key Lime Pie! We shipped our big stuff on a freighter, as planned, parked our car at Bob Straughan's home—and were soon on an Equatoriana night flight to Panama. I can still remember my dreams . . . half awake . . . half asleep . . . droning over the ocean.

At 4 AM, in the nearly-deserted Panama City airport, the lone customs official must have thought we were easy pickings, but, after an hour of haggling, we convinced him we had no money, paid $10 "tax-bribe", and at last were outside, bargaining with a taxi driver. Finally, we agreed on a price to the railroad going across the Isthmus to Atlantic port of Colon, where we would board the ARCABRA to Providence.

In the taxi, silence was abruptly shattered by full-blast Latin music, crashing our eardrums as we thundered north, scattering chickens from the predawn highway! Soon country huts became factories, "Kentucky

Pollo Frito", buzzards on garbage cans, palms and tropical trees in full bloom—it was warm! We stripped down to T-shirts.

Abruptly we arrived at a deserted railway station, only one young police officer was there. He spoke perfect English—we were in the Canal Zone. His friendliness revived us.

The train to Colon through tropical jungle (totally new to us), was spectacular! Just yards away was rain forest, untouched by humans . . . as it had been for thousands of years. Bromeliads by the thousands, each a tropical garden in itself (with a pool of water, many creatures . . . even frogs . . . high in the giant rain forest trees . . . pa rrots . . . even a Toucan!

Soon we were in the English-speaking town of Colon, stopping to record wonderful singing at a tiny church. As we walked the narrow streets between ancient wooden buildings, a sudden tropical downpour sent us under roof overhangs, where laughing—screaming children gleefully showered under gutter-runoffs. Just as suddenly—sunshine again!

We found the tiny Colombian Consul's office, where the secretary took one look at my passport—"born in China"—"no Chinese may go to Colombia," she said, thrusting it back into my hand, ushered us abruptly out the door: "We are closed for two hours." The door closed. We heard the lock snap . . . panic!

"Nema Nanung!" (A Chinese crisis-exclamation, translated: "Now what are we going to do?!") The ARCABRA was to sail in three hours—we had been preparing for a year—Ali was devastated. Bryn wanted to crawl. I was furious, in shock! We went to the nearby park and, desperately, started trying to figure out a realistic solution. Finally, after stomping around the park many times, I realized I must "take the blame", so that the young secretary would not "lose face". I rehearsed. I could do it. I must do it. So much depended on it!

We were waiting at the Consul's door at 2 PM. "I'm sorry, senorita, that I didn't make it clear to you. My parents are US citizens, and I am also. It's just that, by chance, I happened to be born in China where my parents worked. I'm sorry I made you think I was Chinese." She smiled, "That's OK", took my passport in to the Consul. We heard him stamp it. In two minutes we had our visa . . . and were on our way to the dock. (I strongly recommend that travelers get necessary papers well in advance, at big-city Consulates.)

There was the ARCABRA, single engined, low in the water, pretty small for the Atlantic. We met Captain Ulrich, and paid him our fare. There were no cabins or bunks, so we joined the many passengers sitting and lying on the crowded deck. We were on our way—to Old Providence Island!

SEASHELLS & SHARKS—
BEACHCOMBING
WITH OUR BABY

Pumping up our inflatable canoe on the deck of the ARCABRA, we then (as per instructions which came with it) "threw it fearlessly" over the rail into the sea. I climbed down, Ali passed Bryn down to me and followed. We paddled ashore to Capt. Ulrich's yard. Then, with Bryn in her Gerrycarrier on my back, we started walking north to the village of Bailey.

Everything was new, every detail exciting! Boys riding bareback (sometimes with a young brother behind them) green lizards by the thousands, gorgeous flowers in people's yards, friendly smiles. Many walked out to see Bryn and welcome us. Curious children, a boy driving cattle, lime trees and coconuts, others we didn't recognize . . . and always the roar of surf on the reef! Blue-green shallows, patches of coral—we couldn't wait to snorkel! And, up ahead, the Brothers Cays—three islets which we knew were just offshore from Bailey.

Marco had already advised us that Bailey would be a good place to live. We had studied the chart. On the ARCABRA we had met a woman, Carmen, who said she had a nice house in Bailey and was eager to rent us a room—what luck!

An occasional man with machete greeted us—off to the hills to work at family vegetable plot. A fisherman in dugout, throwing his net for "sprat" baitfish. Roosters crowing, almost constantly. Suddenly, a huge green iguana, sunning on a rock, scuttled up a coconut tree! Children in school uniforms stopping to pick fruit. As we passed a truckload of men working on the rocky dirt road, their foreman greeted us, introducing himself as "Alvaro Howard", later to become a lifelong friend.

The cays were close now, out from Ironwood Hill, and we heard an engine, soon learning it was Frank Reed's recently-built lobster-freezing plant in Bailey.

"Where is Carmen's house?" we asked a young girl. "Right there!" she grinned, pointing across the road to a frame house painted green. We climbed a flight of steps, with a porch all around. Soon we had a room, "just for one night", because it was much nicer than we had expected, more expensive than we could afford longterm.

After breakfast we met Frank and Jo Reed, from Florida, in their little concrete house. While sharing island news, they offered us a room till we could find a permanent place. Their most interesting news, to us, was about the house next door to the freezing plant. It was empty. Two women had recently died there and no one wanted to move in. We were off to explore it.

There were two rooms plus a tiny cookshed on downwind south end (like all the older island homes). It was unpainted wood, no glass windows (only wood shutters.) On the outside wall, stamped in black letters was: DDT and a number. ((We learned later that a doctor had sprayed every house on the island with DDT, an early experiment.) Corrugated rusty iron roof fed rainwater into a 55-gallon drum, no toilet (or even outhouse), crawlspace littered with broken bottles and junk. Outside the front door, facing the NE trade wind, was a huge table on sturdy legs set in the ground, with bench—where we were to spend many happy hours.

The yard was overgrown with tall grass, but there was a lime tree with limes, coconut palms, other unknown trees. Happily, for us, it was completely fenced, with locking gate to the road. Bryn could safely crawl. Could we get it for $25 a month, we secretly wondered? That was all we could afford.

I immediately was off to town to see the owner, a retired sea captain. "Yes, I will rent it—would $4 a month be OK?" Jubilantly, I ran most of the way back—"home!"

Now our top priorities were: to get a bed, dig a latrine, find a baby-sitter—so we could go snorkeling!

Claringdon Newball down the road heard about the newcomers with a baby, and loaned us a mattress! Right next door lived twelve year old Amanda Archbold who was eager to take care of Bryn! The latrine I quickly dug in far corner of our yard was one of the first in the neighborhood.

We quickly put the raft together with neighbor boys Dario and John watching. Now we could go snorkeling!

As the days passed we gradually became a part of the Bailey, Rocky Point community. Without refrigerators or supermarkets, we slowly learned the day-by-day self-sufficient life. Ali would walk down the road asking neighbors if they had an extra egg, slowly getting one here and one there. Often she would be given an orange, a banana, a half loaf of bread.

Bartering was common, eggs for a fish, part of a freshly slaughtered pig for some cloth to make a child's dress. When an animal was slaughtered, word was passed around so each family could come and get what they needed for one day. Cut up in the cool of sunrise, it would all be gone within the hour.

Sometimes when I speared two fish in one day, we would have something to barter. But when weather was bad, we would run out of food, and were reduced to buying canned fish or Spam at the little store down the road.

Neighbors walking past on the road would stop at our fence calling out, "Bryn, hi Bryn!".

With no electricity we learned to enjoy the stars. The first satellites were being sent up in those years (1965), so in early evening we watched them pass across the sky, often two or three in an hour, disappearing into the earth's shadow before they reached the horizon.

Often waking late at night we would sit for awhile at our outdoor table to gaze at the stars, soon learning that we could tell time by watching the handle of the Big Dipper revolve like the hour hand of a clock. We thought of the shepherds of old, "watching their flocks by night", naming the stars.

For the three of us, those were wonderful days and nights, becoming part of the community life of Old Providence Island!

BOB MARX—AND TREASURE

Sir Robert Marx, undoubtedly the world's most famous treasure—hunter-archiologist, spent some time on Providence in 1964-65. He was knighted by the Spanish government for reenacting the first voyage of Columbus in a replica of the Nina.

We had read some of his stories (he joked that, not finding enough treasure, he made his living writing books) so we wrote him with questions about seashells and where to live on Providence. His reply hinted that he assumed we were treasure hunters, an assumption made by many islanders also. Eventually islanders became convinced that our interest was marine biology, diving for shells and pleasure. We enjoy "treasure hunting" only in an armchair reading Bob Marx's books.

In my hand right now is a copy of SKIN DIVER, April 1982, with Bob Marx on the cover, coins in one hand and a metal detector in the other. It's not surprising that a few pages further is an article promoting that brand of underwater detector! It's likely that Bob's articles have sold many products, but have not led to finding of any treasure by his readers.

The morning we arrived in Providence he was on the dock to meet us, but was leaving the next day, so our acquaintance lasted only five minutes. The first thing he said (giving us a jolt) was: "Providence is the most shell-less island I've ever seen." It proved true that the beaches are not rich with shells, like some in Florida, but we knew there would be shells hidden in special habitats. Anyway, we came for the island, not just seashells.

Bob told us the house he and his wife had rented would be available, but it was too expensive for us. So Bob, wishing us a good time on Providence, left to pack, while we stayed on the ARCABRA as it continued around to the east side, anchoring in front of Captain Ulrich's home.

Every Caribbean island has treasure stories. Travel brochure writers love to dramatize them and encourage tourists to have fantasies of finding gold coins under every coconut tree. Undoubtedly, every island has its share of wrecks, some with treasure, but if someone seriously tries to hunt, they usually get into quick trouble with authorities—whose concerns are quite different from travel agents.

But, Bob was, admittedly, a real treasure hunter—having devoted years to it, going to virtually every island in the West Indies, and getting into trouble with Government authorities in the Bahamas and elsewhere. But it is also true that he actually did make a living—writing books.

We soon were told by Frank Reed and others, that Bob worked long and hard at searching for treasure, both around the island and at the uninhabited banks to the north. He taught "Bandit" (Bertram Fernandez) to use flippers-mask-snorkel, becoming the first island diver, and soon a lifelong most special friend of mine. Bob took him to Quito Suena bank. There, for hours, day after day, he towed Bandit behind the boat to look for wrecks. "I was shark-bait", Bertram says!

Some islanders, James Rankin in particular, tried to keep an eye on Bob's doings—possibly hoping he might lead them to treasure. Bob, however, when he heard that "the Duke" might be spying on him with a telescope, gave him (I heard) a "bottoms-up" view.

Possibly the biggest influence Bob Marx may have had on Providence was the introduction of diving. In traditional Caribbean culture fishermen didn't go in the water. Many couldn't swim. They fished with hand lines, looking down through glass-bottomed buckets, or boxes.

When we arrived there were more and more young men spearing fish and lobster with spring guns (spear attached by a line), flippers and mask. Many did not use snorkels. None used weight-belts. (On other islands the new breed of diver-fishermen used "Hawaiian slings" with spears unattached, or sometimes, as in Belize, a short rod with large hook on the end to snag lobsters.)

There had been other treasure hunters at Providence earlier, as at all islands. Most went home poorer (like the gold rush '49ers) who left everything for the lust for gold. I guess there will be others. But Bob Marx did leave a very valuable legacy, diving with flippers and mask. Did he take any treasure with him? I guess only he and his wife know.

Those who would like to learn more about Bob Marx's amazing life can Google; Resume, Robert Marx; Discover Jamaica, Historic Port Royal; and Classic Dive Books, Interview with Robert Marx.

Have I personally ever found any treasure, by accident? No . . . in all my 63 years of diving (like most other divers) I've never found even one single coin. Have I ever seen any "treasure" at Providence? Yes . . . James Rankin's son, Pacho, showed me three gold coins found on Old Town beach, and let me photograph them in his hand (see photo). Maybe they were lost in the sand one evening by some of Aury's men gambling on the beach? (See chapter on Luis Aury) Pacho told me years later that he let someone take them "to find their value". They left, and were never heard from again. Gold comes . . . and goes . . . mostly, goes.

There lurks somewhere in every man the desire to get something for nothing. They will sacrifice family and friends, travel to the ends of the earth, daydream night and day, lose their job, risk their life time and again . . . to try to get something for nothing. Treasure hunting and gambling are extreme examples.

The lust for treasure can be almost as dangerous to one's health and happiness as drug addiction, or drug running. Marine biology is infinitely more fascinating, safe, and rewarding. As an amateur naturalist you will find joyful satisfaction, exciting insight, and high adventure—all without endangering your life, friends, or family.

CHRISTMAS MORNING SERENADE

It was a complete surprise to us when, early Christmas morning before breakfast, about twenty young men suddenly came down the road, and right into our yard . . . singing! . . . with guitars and many simple rhythm instruments, including the traditional island jawbone-of-an-ass—with a stick to rattle across the teeth. They gathered around us with greetings and laughter. Bryn was enthralled! They carried her around, passing her from one to another, let her play with the jawbone.

This was a trick-or-treat serenade, they told us, an island custom, young men of each community going from house to house on Christmas morning. We felt privileged to be so quickly accepted as part of the community!

I wondered what the "trick" would be. They certainly gave us a treat, singing a few more songs. Then I found out. They each kissed Ali, and, with "best wishes" and "Merry Christmas!", went on their way. Bryn wanted to go with them!

We didn't yet know that many of these young men were soon to become special friends.

Sun still low, Man-of-War birds circling in the sparkling morning blue sky, ever-present roar of surf on the reef, roosters crowing, the northeast trade wind rustling through our coconut trees—charmed and happy, with wonderful music on our battery-operated shortwave radio, we settled down for Christmas breakfast. Fresh-squeezed orange juice, just-laid scrambled eggs from free-ranging hens, thick slices from Ali's own first fresh-baked island bread, sugar cookies from Miss Picolla . . . and . . . mangoes!

Talking quietly of our families and friends, we thought of the manger in Bethlehem, and of the babies being born right at this very moment, around the world—three each second! As the years have passed we like to think of Christmas as the celebration of the birth of . . . every baby.

We wish you could have joined us that beautiful cool morning on Old Providence Island as from halfway around the world the British Broadcasting Company filled our coconut grove with the Hallelujah Chorus!

FRANK REED—
LOBSTERS & DIVERS

With Bob Marx and wife gone, Frank and Jo Reed were the only visitors on Providence when we arrived. They were wonderful and generous friends. They had come a few years before from Florida (where Frank was in the freezer business) to catch, freeze, and export lobsters. They lived in a small concrete house (like many of the newer ones on the island) and had built a freezing plant next door, with generator. Our house was just 100 yards south, so we had an almost constant roar. They had a 30-foot lobster boat, traps, two aluminum outboard boats, and Kelly (an islander) as full-time jack-of-all-trades. I learned later that similar entrepreneurs were building freezing plants on many islands.

Frank had not had much success with Florida-type traps designed for sandy flats. In Providence maybe it would be less work and bring in more money to hire freelance divers to spear lobsters hiding under coral, paying them a set price per lobster. This plan was now booming, with more and more young men learning to dive and earning more than they had ever dreamed of, more even than Dr. Connally (the only island doctor) or even the alcalde (mayor)!

Later, when I worked four years collecting and harvesting for Upjohn, I saw this happening on many islands. At that time they could easily bring in 25-30 lobsters a day from shallow water. Later they might get 2-3 in a day of difficult 60-foot diving outside the reef.

Overfishing was rampant, the freezer plant owners sadly not protecting the female lobsters in egg-laying season, and doing little to help the young divers open bank accounts, or learn to save. Possibly, at that time, they tended to pay too much, thinking mostly of the export price. Maybe there was no way such fishing could be done for the best benefit of everyone, with no cooperatives as yet, or environmental-protection knowledge or regulations.

So . . . the divers worked . . . a little . . . when they felt like it, bought expensive boomboxes and "stuff", eventually (as available lobsters declined) ending up fairly poor—a familiar sad story, around the world.

I recommend an excellent article from Belize which would apply to Providence: www.ambergriscaye.com/pages/goodscv/lobster.html

A second interesting article deals with the possibility of raising lobsters in captivity—lobster culture: www.poseidonsciences.com/lobster.html

Living next door, and snorkeling everyday ourselves, we got to know many of the divers, who became good friends during our many visits over the next 30 years.

We heard interesting stories about their exploits. Willesley killed a 175-pound "Junefish" with a single shot to the back of its head. He usually tries to hit them an inch behind the eye. "If you punch out their eyes they charge around and can easily mash you." At Queena he saw a 900-pound Jewfish. Divers took one look around rock, and got the hell fast back in the boat—a sea monster—"he could easy eat you!"

I can believe it. They had no scales to check the 900 pounds, but I have no doubt it was big enough to be dangerous to a diver. In SKIN DIVER about 1960 there was a story: "I was swallowed by a giant fish."

OSCAR

If you had visited Providence in the 1960's it would not have been long before you met Oscar. In his sixties, shabby clothes, carrying bags of old cans and bottles, an ancient worn-down machete, battered pack of cigarettes, cooking pot, a piece of fish . . . He had no home, wandering the island night and day, picking up discarded items (sometimes, not discarded).

He would introduce himself as professor Oscar Newball Bryan, island "sanitary commissioner." His speech was often reminiscent of Shakespeare or the Bible. "I put Newball first in respect for my mother. It was she who has done the most to wipe the shades of ignorance from my eyes." I will always remember that beautiful tribute. "She is over in the cemetery there, a few years now, but I still remember somehow what she thinks . . . and when I go to the extreme, I have something yet to hold me. Well, I'm bad, but not vicious.

I've been trying to relieve the street and country here of some of the broken glass and nails. Well, I guess it's good for the tire men! The downfall of one man is the uprising of another. I've been doing this work a long time, but can't be appreciated."

Oscar could be warm, friendly, courteous, sitting for hours delighting children with stories and songs—yet, if you did him an injustice, his wrath was quick and violent.

You might see him sitting under a tree reading, or walking the road barefoot at noon in sweltering sun, picking up broken glass. In church he might rise from the back pew to speak powerfully in a voice full of feeling. Again, the formality of the church suddenly angering him, he would mutter: "hypocrites!"

Known as the island madman, though usually quite rational, there were times when he earned his reputation. Once we were wakened at dawn by Oscar's loud voice. There he was in our yard with a papaya and flowers in a chamber pot, starting to plant it. Obviously he had dug it up from someone else's garden. Later that day that someone sent a boy, saying we could keep the papaya and the flowers, but she would like her chamber pot back.

When he first met Bryn Oscar pulled out a stubby pencil, old notebook and wrote her an original poem. Wish I had it now to share with you.

When not invited in by the Reeds early one morning he flew into a rage, hacking branches off a tree in their yard, raving loudly about the faults of North Americans—then came to the door to ask sheepishly: "Any hard feelings, Mrs. Reed?" At times he was like an Old Testament prophet, blasting people who considered themselves "good."

Another time when Oscar may have picked up something not "discarded" was when one of my marine biology groups was in the new three-story Hotel Aury. My room on ground floor had a window easily reached from the street. I was reading a fascinating book, CULTURE AGAINST MAN, by anthropologist, Jules Henry, keeping it on the window sill. I heard Oscar's voice, then noticed that the book was gone. I hope you enjoyed it, Oscar, as much as I did.

Later in the week, at dawn one morning, we were awakened by Oscar's booming voice, proclaiming and "preaching" from the street below. Our marine biologist went to the window and let him have it, shouting his anger. Later he admitted this didn't do any good, "but it sure helped to get it off my chest!" Trying to salvage some of my group's much-needed sleep, I rushed down to the street to join Oscar, explaining that with their vigorous daily schedule, they needed every hour of sleep. Oscar replied: "The early bird gets the worm," but, he did quiet down. We talked for a minute. Then I invited him to come back to visit us in late afternoon. He wandered off. I went back to bed.

During another group, when we were staying across the street on the second floor above Mr. Ray Howard's store, we were startled one night after supper to hear a woman's voice calling out from the roof of the hotel. A mentally unstable airline hostess from San Andres had slipped into a psychotic state, stripped, and crawled out the third floor window, and was standing naked high on the tile roof, in full view of the main town street. In a loud voice she proclaimed that she might jump, and was thirsty.

My group crowded to the porch, amazed, excited. Almost all, including our marine biologist, assumed she was a sex-flaunting street-walker, a "bad" woman. I suggested that, instead, she was mentally ill, suffering deeply from guilt, confusion, and a very painful childhood. She was a desperately sick woman.

A small group of men had gathered on the street below her. One, in a calm authoritative voice, said reassuringly: "Don't jump. We will get you some water. Everything is all right." Finally, she crawled back through the window, and was taken to the hospital in San Andres next day. If Oscar had been there, I wonder what he would have said.

Oscar was occasionally angry, though I never heard of him doing any serious harm to anyone. I did hear that sometimes, when kids taunted and tormented him, he threw stones and even threatened them with a fishhook, maybe the saddest chapter in his life.

Usually Oscar was mild and friendly. Ali tells of a time when she was sitting on the steps of the alcaldia (town hall) with Bryn, when Oscar came by. He sat down beside them, took Bryn in his lap and told her stories. He was very tender. Bryn was charmed. I wish I had a picture and a recording.

Once when we were riding home from town in a pickup (the only "bus service") Oscar was on the bench opposite us, expertly weaving the end of a rope, from his years of experience on sailing ships. He had many skills, was full of surprises.

Without any doubt, Oscar knew the island more intimately than anyone, wandering night and day (getting some food from friends and relatives), talking with newcomers. He knew nearly every family and their history. A scientist who came to research island society, wrote a book about him.*

One morning in January, 1967 as I started around the island with my tape recorder, I found Oscar sitting on the rocks at water's edge scrubbing his gnarled callused feet, cleaning a mild infection. I gave him a tube of antibiotic ointment which I always carried. "Walking barefoot, I have so little ambition as a shoemaker." I asked if I could take a photo. He said yes and immediately put on a red checked shirt from his paper bag, and began smoothing down his hair. I took two pictures.

Then I said that I had better get going, do it "now", if I was to record more life stories before the Arcarbra sailed tomorrow. He laughed: "Well, you know they say the Pharaoh was a Spaniard." "How's that Oscar?" "When Moses asked the Pharaoh when he would like the plague to end, he answered, tomorrow. . . . manyana!" We both laughed.

On my way down the west shore I was thinking of the philosophy of skepticism, deeply ingrained in the islanders. For generations Providence has been the "end of the line", an almost forgotten possession of a distant large mother country which already had enough problems right at home. With a different climate, different ethnic background, different religion, even a different language and culture, not to speak of poor communications—promises made were seldom carried out. Islanders rightfully were skeptics. They would believe it when they saw it.

In late afternoon we met again. How about telling me your life story, Oscar?

"I was born right here, in Rocky Point, left at 14 to Bocas. They had a farm down there, cocoplum. I worked there for a few months. Then I contracted blackwater fever, came back and almost died. Yes, there was just a step between me and death.

There were no cars in those days, first was Mr. Philip Bryan's, brother of Elijah Bryan. A couple of boys got drunk and run it in

---

*   Wilson, Peter J., OSCAR: An Inquiry Into the Nature of Sanity, Random House, NY, 1947

the ditch. After the fever I sailed on some boats, the Brinton, the Philadelphia, the Cinques Hermanos that later became the Excelsior. They were all sailing boats. Then I went to the Navy, on the Condonera Onic ?, a battleship, for one year, went to Bogota for ten weeks, then joined the Onic in Baranquilla. I was 37, that was in 1935, and I was about 198 pounds. (dates mixed?} Then I came back to the island and kind of settled down, back and forth to St. Andrews, and I studied in Panama, graduated from the 9th grade over there, then took higher studies in the Canal Zone, at an American training school, professor C.J. Boyd.

I have been suffering right through all along. I guess I didn't travel up like the other boys did, and made good, some of them . . . but somebody has to be at the home base. The boys, you know, go out and get a preparation, and then they want to come back, but the island is too small for them.

Chance is the biggest industry now, able-bodied men walking up and down, nicely dressed, wanting you to pay for a chance. Anybody who wants to can get a book and sell numbers.

I doubt they will ever finish the airport. They are not engineers, they are simple men. If airfield had been given as a contract we would have an airfield long before now, but these people have not the spirit of push. They just draw their month's pay and go home, you know, and feel that's all in life.

I've been living on the land for quite a time now, so I plan to build a house. There are plenty of bricks around town there that are not being used. I meant to start it in November, but I kept busy at this and that, and neglect myself. But I find I'm getting older . . . I once had a woman 8 years, and then I was experimenting to find another one for forty years now! (chuckle) But I'm getting older, and I guess I'll need someone to take care of me, so I may have to take another woman. I have built three houses already, but I seldom live in them (embarrassed laugh) I enjoy outdoor life. I have some cultivation (garden) I used to follow up, but it's over a year now I've neglected that . . . I may be around here for a day or two, three or four . . . "

Oscar wandered off, barefooted, down the dusty dirt road he had walked so often.

An island is the world in miniature . . . one night I had a fantasy that, like Oscar, I might become an "island clean-up man." They now call it conservation of Nature. Oscar has wandered on now, out of this life, but all of us who wish to can improve our own lives from his experience. Thank you, Oscar, for helping to "wipe the shades of ignorance" from our eyes.

Note: I wrote the above before reading Peter Wilson's book.

IGUANAS, HIKITI, BOA, BAT HOLES & COCKSPUR

Soon we discovered we had an iguana, right in our yard! It was three and a half feet long, several shades of gorgeous green—majestic, the king of our neighborhood. He lived among the coconuts, high in one of our palms.

One day I saw him sunning himself on a flat rock in the scrubby grass, right in the middle of our yard. I decided to get a dramatic shot with our 8mm movie camera, so I crawled slowly to a good spot. He didn't move. Then I carefully tossed a rock so it would land behind him, hoping he would come right toward me. He did! With the camera humming, his head soon filled the entire viewfinder! It was a high point in the life of a very amateur photographer.

At that time there were many iguanas on Providence. Young men would go out in a morning and catch 6-8 to ship off to San Andres. A smaller species was black, more aggressive and (I heard) capable of biting. There may be others.

Several types of small lizards are far more numerous. Within minutes of arriving on Providence you begin to see them, sunning on rocks by the roadside, displaying on every bush, with bobbing heads and dramatically expanded throat pouches underneath.

At breakfast one morning, we were surprised to find a land turtle crossing our yard. It was about 8-inches long, with handsome yellow and brown markings. We had fun playing with it for a few days, learned from our neighbors that it was called "Hikiti", then let it go on its way.

There were pigeons which islanders shot for food. Occasionally we saw a dead snake on the road, maybe four or five feet long, the "chicken boa". We never heard of any poisonous snakes. We did hear talk of wild pigs, but never saw one, and can't confirm that they existed.

In the streams there were crayfish, and freshwater fish. We wondered what their history was. How did they get to Providence? That fascinating story will someday be told by some researcher, maybe you.

Two caves, at opposite ends of the island, are called "Bat Holes". The first we explored is on the northwest corner of Catalina. We could snorkel right into its dramatic large entrance, easily visible from boats a mile away. It does not extend very far into the cliff, probably formed by ocean waves when the sea was higher rather than underground water flowing out. It had a few bats, but we were more intrigued by the tide pools on the floor of the cave, where we found anemones, fish, crabs, starfish, octopus, shells, and hundreds of creatures and plants yet unknown to us—a beautiful and fascinating place.

The other was far from us at the SW point, harder to enter, so, when two young friends invited us to go, we were excited. We found our flash camera and filled a lantern with kerosene. They told us there were two ways to enter, from a boat, or climbing down a short cliff from the road. We went by boat, the easiest way except when the sea is rough. It was a little tricky climbing from the boat to slippery rocks, but once in the small cave mouth we saw bats hanging all over the ceiling. Some, disturbed by us, started flying. There were many near misses, but none hit us. The floor, covered with guano, wound slowly upwards over rough rocks. Climbing gingerly up, hundreds of bats now swirling around us, we made it, with our lantern, maybe a hundred feet in, or more. The cave mouth was no longer visible. It was quite dark. Soon it became so narrow we could go no further. We saw no running water, no stalactites, so apparently this cave also had been made by waves. We heard there might be snakes, but didn't see them, or any other creature. Of course on this amateur exploration we didn't observe very carefully. A bit disappointed, but very glad we came, we were off for home, to take baths in our little galvanized washtub.

A tiny "fire ant" has a powerful sting for its size. If you happen to stand on their nest, they will quickly swarm up your legs, biting as they climb. They were in our yard in one sandy area. Bryn, being an adventurous crawler, went everywhere so it was a challenge to keep her away from that spot.

Two more serious hazards of Old Providence are Manganeel and Cockspur. Manganeel is a tree with poisonous leaves, growing only along the shore. It can give you terrible sores, ruining your sleep for a week. Found throughout the West Indies, it's a tree important to learn to recognize. Manganeel Bay, isolated on the southeast shore, has a beautiful secluded beach, no houses in our time. Now it is known as a "hippy hangout."

"Cockspur", a species of acacia with huge thorns (known as Bullhorn acacia) has large and very aggressive stinging ants living inside the thorns. For over a hundred years scientists have known of "ant-plants" as home for only one species of ant, which live nowhere else. It is widespread on Providence and has been called the "island's best defense". The ants chew a small hole at the base of each thorn and live inside, but crawl over every branch right out to the very tips, ready to leap "vengefully" onto any creature that might brush past. If you are the victim, it will be sadly memorable, again with lost sleep, and pain for hours, or days.

As is true for so many species, scientists have discovered in recent years that there is a symbiotic relationship, cockspur and ants each benefiting the other. The cockspur leaves produce sugar and protein eaten by the ants, who in turn drive away insects and other creatures that might try to eat the plant. The ants also kill strangler vines which start to grow on the cockspur. Sadly, between people and cockspur there is no benefit for either one.

Many species, having slowly changed over thousands of years, are now unique, indigenous to Old Providence. No one yet knows how many. A seashell, the "Roosevelti", was first found here when US President Franklin D. Roosevelt stopped to fish in 1938. In 1967 I talked with an elderly islander who remembered talking with him at the dock in town. He had a scientist on board who made a quick survey.

During one of my Adventures in Marine Biology in August 1972, an almost white Hamlet fish was found in Providence for the first time (see photo by Ben Rose). The Indigo Hamlet of similar size and shape is widespread in the Caribbean. I don't know if it has since been seen anywhere else, or scientifically named as a new species. It may be "a color variation." We named it, unofficially, the "Providence Hamlet". It's not common, but you may be one of the lucky ones to see it.

One morning I decided to climb the Peak (2000-ft), foolishly not getting advice. Ali wisely chose to stay home. So, off I went, starting up the nearest track which seemed to head towards the Peak. Along a small stream, bromiliads on trees, birds singing, it was easy hiking and beautiful! I wished Ali had come. Going through several barbed wire fences, passing little vegetable-plots, carefully closing all gates, I finally came to a three-way branch. Unable to see the Peak anymore, I chose what I felt was the right track. It led to another mini-farm, but the track went no further. I went back to try the second branch, but once again it ended at another plot. The third also ended at another mini-farm.

So, undaunted as yet, I started up through the waist-high bush, encouraged because the Peak was again visible, as well as some high grass areas. I would keep going till I got to that grass. Of course there was Cockspur and other thorns. The mountain got rougher, boulders under the bushes an increasing hazard. Several times I fell between them, disappearing under the bushes. This was not so great. I was bleeding in a dozen places. I stood on a rock, looking up at the Peak, still a long way off. I hated to give up, even dreaded going back the way I came, but it seemed the wisest thing. Admitting defeat, I struggled back, finally getting home just before supper—bruised, bitten, scratched, and bleeding—to tend my wounds.

We soon learned that the majority of tracks go only to private family farms. You have to know the ones going all the way. Later, with a guide, we did climb all the way to the peak going up one side of the island along a stream, then through mammoth seven-foot-high grass on the high hills. Then we walked though an easy grassy valley, pristine and beautiful, probably like this for thousands of years. Finally, the Peak, a magnificent view . . . hills, lagoon, reef, and ocean!

Starting down the east side, we stopped at the lookout spot where Regnier (the German spy during WW-II) had his radio to tell U-boats of passing ships. Continuing down, we ended at the home of Miss Rachel (James Rankin's sister and Regnier's wife), amazed to find she had a piano, and a huge glass-doored cabinet of beautiful chinaware. When we first arrived, she had sent a boy over with a cup of fresh milk, not knowing that Ali was still nursing Bryn. Ali went to thank her, and visited many times. She said Regnier was a very cultured German. A beauty in her youth, she was now lonely. Loving to cook, she sent food daily to James by a boy on horseback. The story (true or not) was that he ate only her food, being afraid that someone might poison him.

So, learning more and more about LIFE on Old Providence, our own lives grew daily more fascinating and enriched.

DRIFTING AND SAILING
TO NICARAGUA

On a long walk south one day, past Capt. Ulrich's house, we met the Newball family who played a key role in developing the island's Adventist schools. We heard the terrifying true story of their two young sons who accidentally drifted away from the island . . . to Nicaragua.

On the west side of Providence there is no barrier reef, only a few patch reefs. Along the shore, in the lee of the island, it is calm, protected from the trade winds by the mountains. But, out a quarter of a mile, the wind curls down over the hills to touch the sea once again.

The boys, out fishing or paddling for fun, suddenly found themselves out too far, caught in the wind, drifting west away from the island. Paddling as hard as they could, they were still moving west. The wind was too much for them. They could see the island but no one on shore could see them now, and no one had noticed they were in trouble. They were out at sea, a little-traveled area, only Corn Island and Nicaragua ahead . . . 150 miles away.

They had no food or water. Night came. Then another day . . . another night. Finally a distant shore, through the surf onto the beach. They had made it!

They were sent home by Nicaraguan officials. Over the years we came to know them. Lynn became a doctor in San Andres, his wife a marine biologist. He was shot on the streets of Bogota. Probably no one knows the whole story.

Another friend, Bartlett, (now an island businessman), also made a trip to Nicaragua. One day when he was young (for personal reasons that only he knows) he took his father's catboat, and sailed to Nicaragua. He also made it safely . . . and was sent home.

If you come to Providence you can ask him personally for the whole story: what he took with him, how many days and nights he sailed, the weather, where he landed (probably also through the surf onto a beach), why he went. He may not tell everything, and I doubt if he will recommend it as a good way to go to Nicaragua, even though memorable, exciting, inexpensive, and without a visa.

I once typed up some messages with my address, offering a small reward, sealed one hundred in tiny bottles with wax, and tossed them overboard from the ARCABRA coming from San Andres. I got one reply, an interesting letter from a fisherman in Nicaragua—written by his priest. It helped me better understand the anguish of poverty.

We did almost all our diving on the eastside, and, when we used a motor we usually went directly into the wind, so that if the motor failed, we would drift right back home. When we did go on the lee side, we always were careful to stay very close to shore in water shallow enough to anchor if the motor failed—which it sometimes did.

So, we missed out on the adventure of drifting to Nicaragua.

MUSIC . . . AND DANCING

Providence islanders love music and dancing. Almost every home has a guitar player. Songs have been composed here . . . like "Uncle Bug is Under the Reef." Several small groups play at dances, including Willie B who is wonderful on the mandolin. The bass was made from an inverted galvanized washtub, a vertical broomstick attached with a cord from center of tub to top of stick. When cord was held taught and plucked, it made a nice reverberation in the tub, much like a bass fiddle. There was always a jawbone with stick to rattle across the teeth, and, of course, gourd maracas. Sometimes just two musicians, guitar and mandolin, made wonderful music, a bottle of island rum beside them.

A most interesting thing about dancing in Providence is that traditional English dances have become part of the culture, enjoyed through the years, probably a legacy from Jamaican ancestors. At every party a schottische will be played. Occasionally a group will give a concert of dances in old English dress.

We were soon invited to small parties in homes. Sadly, I'm a very poor dancer . . . (except for square dancing and international folk dancing. Ali and I first met at Folkdance House in New York City!) Ali, on the other hand, is an excellent dancer—so, when all the men wanted to dance with her, I was a bit sad and jealous. Let's be honest—very sad and jealous!—my problem . . . We were still almost newly-weds.

So, my very strong advice to all parents is: "teach your children well"—to learn to dance, and to play the piano or guitar, from a very young age.

Music and dancing are, of course, part of LOVE—the very heart of LIFE. Providence islanders know that, deep in their souls.

During the years of Adventures in Marine Biology we had some great parties, with many islanders attending. The last time I saw Willie B, in 1998, he smiled wistfully: "Yes, when your groups were here, we had some wonderful parties!"

SATURDAY HORSE RACES & GREASED PIG CHASE

We heard there were exciting horse races on Saturdays, so, taking the long walk down to Southwest Bay, we found a huge crowd already there. With impromptu music, singing, and laughter—it was a picnic-fiesta day-at-the-races!

Owners proudly led their favorite horses up and down the beach. Jockeys were barefoot boys, usually sons of the owners. The first race was about to start—three horses, jockeys bareback—bets being made. This was serious business, not just for fun. All eyes were now on the horses—they're off!—to the end of the long beach, and return. As they came back in sight, excitement surged, reaching a deafening peak. At the finish, there were silent glum faces, lost amid ear-splitting shouts from the victors. One very proud jockey was the happiest boy on the island, his status in the community up quite a few notches.

Between races there was a greased-pig chase, with young men competing. This was hilarious! The crowd made a tight circle, their legs making a fence, while the piglet was carefully well greased. Released, it ran like a rabbit! As more bets were made, the young men made diving tackles, tried to scoop it up in their arms, or grab one leg with both hands, but there was only failure for a long time. Finally, success! Covered with scratches and bruises, the winner presented the violently struggling-squeeling piglet, tight in his arms, for the crowd's approval. I'm sure it was soon a feast for family, relatives, and neighbors.

Equally exciting were frequent catboat sailing races, held on the eastside, usually ending in town. Once again, bets ran high. On a brisk NE tradewind day, spray flying, you could see an almost constant stream of water from the gourd bailer. As always, the fine arts of sailing were fascinating and exciting—how far to go before tacking, how to avoid the calm in the lee of an island, how best to skirt the shallow reefs, choosing just the right angle to get through the narrow channel into the harbor. Sometimes heated disputes broke out at the finish. I never could understand exactly what it was all about.

A few years later, members of my Adventures in Marine Biology groups often joined the races, one in each boat. They were welcomed, especially the girls of course.

So, we were learning there was a lot happening on Old Providence beyond work . . . music, dancing, races . . . Does it make you want to come? You will be welcomed!

WANDERERS—DO YOU HAVE A BIG SISTER?

In the '60's, tourists seldom found their way to Providence, but an occasional adventurer would wander in.

A message from the Alcalde (the mayor), one day, said the US consul and his wife were visiting from Bogota and asked me to show them around. So I took them, in my plain little fiberglass boat with 5-hp outboard, out past Morgan Head and around Catalina, passing old cannon on the rocks where they had been abandoned years ago. They were surprised to hear that the US had once had the chance to buy this island, but turned it down.

Another day, I missed Marlon Brando when he was checking out the world's most beautiful islands, where he might like to live. He finally choose Tahiti.

Occasionally a yacht sailed in, often on its way around the world, from the Panama Canal towards Miami. We showed them our local area charts, which they might not have room to carry, making sure they knew of the many only-partially-explored reefs ahead of them. We always told them especially the story of the Morning Star, sailing their same course, to wreck right here at Point-of-Reef, Old Providence.

An amateur treasure-hunter with metal detector found a cannonball near the fort, and was immediately evicted by authorities.

Two juniorhigh teachers from Washington DC stayed a few weeks, telling us of 14-yr-old students who proudly brought their babies to show off at school, the most "important" thing they had done in their short lives, living in poverty-stricken neighborhoods only a few blocks from the Capitol building.

We heard of a young Frenchman walking around the island asking young girls if they had a big sister. When I met him it was obvious that he was island-hopping, big-sister-to-big-sister. Not being a promoter of unplanned babies, I asked him if he was careful to have a supply of condoms? When he seemed totally unconcerned, I told Ali about him. She was as angry as I, so I found him again and asked him how he would feel if he didn't know who his father was, and his mother was unable to provide him a happy life? In my youthful anger, I told him there is nothing sadder than an unloved baby! . . . that the ARCABRA was sailing the next morning, and he had better be on it, or (bluffing) I would have the authorities deport him. Next day, he was gone.

Of course the most interesting visitors were the members of my groups, Adventures in Marine Biology. I have many letters expressing their gratitude to the island for providing the most wonderful experience of their lives.

OUR SNORKELING ADVENTURES

Our days were becoming a flow of fun, pleasure and new adventures. Before breakfast we began finding a freshly laid egg on our chair cushion each morning. What luck! Free eggs! Maybe tomorrow there will be a golden one! We ate a few, but then began noticing our neighbor's daughter searching all over her yard, and then into ours. We finally realized she was looking for "strangely-missing" eggs. In this self-sufficient no-refrigerator economy, food is eaten day-to-day. Every egg counts. So, we confessed. She was immediately very happy, and from then on was a friendly daily early morning visitor.

Bryn and Amanda were having a ball, so we felt free to paddle off after breakfast for a morning of snorkeling. The three Brothers Cays were closest, so we enjoyed an intensive exploration, going slowly around each one, many times. We found a handsome Trumpet Triton on the nearby grass, out first large shell. What a beauty it was!

One morning we saw something looking out at us from a 6-inch "cave-mouth" in the coral. It was a fairly large eye. We carefully moved closer to peer in. When we moved back and forth, left to right, the eye did the same—obviously carefully watching us! We knew it was not a fish, but what was it? We inched closer. and then suddenly we knew. It was our first octopus, obviously a very intelligent creature.

Another day, on the beach with Bryn and Craig (aged 4 and 2), we found a small octopus in an empty conch shell in the shallows and put it in a bucket, high on the sand, to watch it. Immediately it climbed out and started crawling across the sand straight towards the water. We caught it again, putting the bucket higher up on the beach, behind some rocks. Once again it climbed out immediately, crawling by the shortest path around the rocks, and straight to the water. Could it hear, as well as see?

We tried it again, putting the bucket higher on the beach, behind many rocks close to bushes—would it try escaping into the nearest bush? Oh no! Once again it quickly took the shortest route—to the sea. Very much impressed, we let it go.

Almost everyday I would do a little spear-fishing, so we often came home with a fish or lobster for dinner. It was easy and fun—gourmet luxury in paradise!

One morning peering down through an opening in the top of a big coral head, we found we were looking into a cave, with a large 7-foot Nurse Shark lying there on the sand, motionless, only its gills moving slowly. I reached down through the opening with my spear and could gently touch it with spear-tip, but it hardly moved. We swam all around the coral head finding a large doorway to the cave. There was the shark, way back in there, lying still on the sand—asleep?

We had our movie camera, so I wondered if we could get a spectacular head-on shot as it came swimming out, but we couldn't wait all day. Being "macho", I asked Ali to wait with the camera in front of the cave-mouth, while I went back to the opening to poke it more vigorously. Wives are expendable, especially in the cause of spectacular photography! Having read that Nurse Sharks are comparatively harmless, unless attacked, she grudgingly agreed. It worked! Ali got the film, and survived, the shark passing close by her and then swimming away down the reef.

One unusually calm day, we headed out for the reef, finding some magnificent Elkhorn coral. We spent an hour taking our best pictures. Even as rank amateurs, we couldn't miss here.

Then, nearby, we discovered a narrow gap in the reef, and for the first time, swam through to the outside—suddenly, a different world! The bottom dropped abruptly, from the 10-foot depth inside, to 30 outside. Many different types of fabulous coral, sea fans swaying, new types of fish, some in large schools. Excited, we hovered, looking, trying to take it all in.

Almost under us, was something different, man made. It was a large 4-foot bomb, with fins, unexploded. We learned later that, during World War II the US had stationed a Consolidated PBY Catalina flying boat at Providence to try to bomb passing German U-boats. (For photo and more information about this famous aircraft Google: Warbird Alley: PBY Catalina) Returning, they would drop unused bombs on the reef, for practice, and to avoid possible explosion when landing. Coming towards us was a large shark, swimming slowly. It kept looking bigger. It was our first time outside the reef so "for some reason" we snorkeled slowly back through the reef, to our boat.

On the deeper calm sand flats inside the reef where we seldom snorkeled, because there was "nothing to see", one day we barely spotted two large Queen Conchs. They almost blended into the sand, but their lurching movement caught our eye. We dove down, put them in the boat to add to our collection, and for conch chowder. I can taste it now! The lips of the shells were very large, smooth and undamaged, unlike most conchs, worn down from "crawling" on rougher bottom. Later, the NY Museum of Natural History told us they were the largest conchs and most beautiful they had ever seen. We wished we had kept one, but we do have a picture, with Bryn.

After reading, and sad experience with smelly shells, we had learned how to clean them without cracks, by putting them in a large pot of cold water, bringing it almost to a boil very slowly. (If you plunge a live shell suddenly into boiling water, the shell will develop many tiny cracks.) After boiling, the conch meat can be pulled out easily, without having to chop a small hole to break its grasp (as the islanders do, having no use for the shell). In the islands there are amazingly large piles of shells, hundreds or thousands, from years of harvesting. In recent years, with growth of population and tourism, even juvenile conchs are harvested. Conchs are becoming rare, conch chowder an expensive luxury—a part of our sad worldwide ecological decline.

Back at Brothers Cays another morning, peering in under the coral, we were only three feet from a "South Pacific Lionfish"!

"It couldn't be!", but it surely looked like one! It had long finger-like fins all over it, and was dangerously poisonous—IF it WAS a Lionfish. We never saw it again. Had we discovered a new species? We didn't know enough, and thought we would never know. It was an exciting, eye-to-eye, most-memorable experience! Then, in 2000 I began reading that Lionfish were being discovered in Florida, and even on the coast of the Carolinas. Had they escaped from salt water aquariums? Had their eggs come in bilge water through the Panama Canal? So many have been found that it is probable that a self-sustaining population has developed in the Atlantic. Those who want more information, Google: New Jersey Scuba Diver, Marine Biology, Tropical Fish. You should report all Lionfish sightings to Paula Whitfield, NOAA Beaufort Laboratory (252-728-8714 or e-mail: paula.whitfield@noaa.gov.)

My personal speculation is that maybe some eggs came through the Panama Canal, were picked up by the leaking ARCABRA in Colon, and then while anchored in front of Capt. Ulric's house were ejected when he pumped the bilges—just a few miles from our sighting location. What do you think? Anyway, all divers at Providence should keep a lookout for Lionfish!

Maybe there are no Coelacanth in the deep waters around Providence, but there could be other undiscovered species. Recently another species of Coelacanth was discovered in Indonesia, 10,000 km from the original discovery in the Comoros off Africa. BBC,Sci/Tech,New "living fossil" identified.

We heard many stories from fishermen and sea captains about huge "50-ft" sharks they had seen. Morgan Bush laughingly said: "I didn't stay around to measure it!" These were undoubtedly whale sharks, which swim slowly with their huge mouths open, feeding on plankton and small fish. They are not dangerous to humans. In recent years many divers have snorkeled with them, but we have yet to see one. Can you imagine one appearing in front of you out of the depths at Blue Hole!

Another day, while taking some pictures of color-changes when photographing at different depths, we saw something in the distance coming straight towards us—was it a shark? It was four! Taking no chances, and with limited shark experience at that time, we swam for the boat in record time. Ali, easily the winner, vaulted in ahead of me, but I was close behind. Then I casually remarked: "They weren't so big, probably would have swum slowly on past us." Macho me.

Our most bone-chilling experience ever, was at Lawrence Reef, a short distance NW of the harbor, a very special magnificent place. We had spent a lazy hour exploring the shallows, admiring small fish, each more spectacular than the last, in dazzling sunlight over miniature coral gardens. Heading back to the boat we saw something large and black, not twenty feet away. Was it a log? a sunken dugout canoe? Now, we saw it clearly, as it edged closer, head slightly down. It was clearly a Barracuda—a giant! Of course we saw Barracuda all the time, every hour, and had learned pretty much to ignore them. We had read that the only known attack on a diver was when the diver had speared one—that's logical!

But this one was in a class by itself, maybe 8-feet, very dark. But the most dramatic thing was the thickness of its body, not 6-8 inches like the average large five or six foot Bara. This monster was more like 10-12 inches thick, weighing maybe 200 pounds! I'm trying to be conservative in this "fish story". It will be more believable if you read my friend Bob Straughan's article, "Two Ten-Foot Barracuda Sighted" near Miami, in Skin Diver Magazine, about 1960. The Columbia Encyclopedia says the Great Barracuda may reach ten feet in length.

The giant was still hovering, head down, watching us—encroachers on his territory. We knew better than to turn and flee, so edged slowing backwards toward the boat, keeping our eyes on him. Even today he is sharply clear in our minds. We talk of him occasionally, wondering how big he is now, and how large Barracuda can get. Fish continue to grow throughout their lives. A few years later, Dr. Hunt, a member of my Adventures in Marine Biology group in 1968, saw him again, right at Lawrence Reef: "By far the most dramatic creature I've ever seen!"

So, our days passed, filled with fun, adventure, new experiences— and the always-overwhelming beauty of Nature. Maybe there is no other place like coral reefs where one can so easily plunge into a magnificent world, little changed in thousands of years. We were becoming more and more dedicated to wanting to keep it that way, but were not yet aware of the worldwide ecological threats to our unique blue-green "ocean-planet"—Earth.

We were learning never to touch the coral, certainly not stand on it! Some of my group members (especially wives of marine biologists) were not good at this, but I talked about it every day. When snorkeling or scuba diving, PLEASE touch nothing but water till you return to the boat.

Once beside Catalina on the grass flats between the fort and Morgan's Head, I came upon a ten foot manta ray feeding, doing somersaults one after the other, mouth wide open, scooping in plankton and maybe small fish. There is no record of any sort of attack. On my office wall I have the Feb. 1981 National Geographic photo of Stan Waterman's son Gordy with scuba—riding a manta, holding onto two remoras attached to its back!

One amazing thing about snorkeling is that, even after years, you usually see something new every day that you've never seen before, and then a lifetime may pass without seeing it again. For instance, once in the Bahamas I saw a medium-sized Barracuda with its jaws wide open. He wasn't chomping. It was as if his jaws were locked open at 45 degrees! I watched him for awhile, wondering if he had a "lockjaw" problem. Then as I snorkeled on ahead, I saw a fish struggling on the bottom with a big bite out of its body. It was bleeding. Here was the answer. While the Barracuda was chewing and swallowing that big bite, the fish had escaped and the Barracuda was still hunting, to finish it off.

Actually, it is rare to see Barracuda aggressively hunting, and very rare to see one actually making a kill. They like the foamy area where waves are breaking on the reef, and I have occasionally seen them shooting back and forth in those areas. It makes the snorkeler want to quickly move on to calmer areas!

Once at Andros we snorkeled at a blue hole where Cousteau had dived, looking down in amazement at the tunnel growing smaller and disappearing into the depths. The blue hole was about 50 yards in diameter, and on one side a school of fish were circling under the ledge. We quickly noticed that several barracuda were making dashes at the fish, and possibly even had the fish hemmed in against the wall. Feeling a little uncomfortable, we left.

Later that day we were snorkeling up a creek back to where our car was parked, when we noticed a large barracuda following us. We had been followed by barracuda hundreds of times, as all snorkelers have, but this one was following a bit too closely and too persistently, moving up till it was a bare ten feet behind our flippers.

We knew Barracuda don't attack snorkelers, but we couldn't help wondering if we were about to become the exception. I guess every snorkeler has sometime wondered this! We were especially concerned because Ali had a scratch on her knee . . . so we had to admit we were quite happy finally to crawl out by our car.

Another one-time barracuda experience was during the last week of August, 1960, when Bob Straughan, saltwater aquarium expert from Miami, was our leader. We were outside the reef at Andros, when we came upon uncountable thousands of young barracuda, all swimming south in a seemingly unending school. The visibility was at least 100 feet, but we couldn't see any beginning or end of the school. They were all the same size, about 16 inches long. Bob has also written about this in one of his books. He has probably spent more hours snorkeling than I, many thousands, and he had never seen anything like this before.

It makes me wonder if there is a place where Barracuda go to spawn, hatching millions at one time and place. Then, for safety, the young travel together. Maybe someone will check this out and once again see an August migration. Please don't accept this theory as fact. It is just an interesting speculation. Maybe you will be the one to research it. If so, let me know!

In Puerto Escondido, Mexico, going far out to swim with wild dolphins, we often see huge floating logs, with a whole little world of creatures around it. I would guess that algae, barnacles, and seaweed grow first, which begin to attract tiny fish, more and more. These bring small predators, then finally Mahi Mahi and sharks. A self-sustaining community has slowly grown, far out at sea!

One thing I know for certain—on your future snorkeling adventures in marine biology, you will see things I have never seen. I envy you!

SPECIAL ADVENTURES WITH JORN GEISTER

One summer, as I was passing through San Andres preparing for an Adventures in Marine Biology group, I was lucky to meet a German graduate student specializing in coral reefs, Jorn Geister. Realizing he would be a great asset to our group, I invited him to join us. All of us, especially myself, learned a great deal from him—and will continue learning, into the future. He is now professor of coral reef geology in Bern, Switzerland, and visits Providence occasionally.*

My first vivid memory of Jorn, was when our group was diving near the edge of Blue Hole. At that time Jorn had not been trained in scuba, but was a superb free diver. He spotted a giant "Jewfish" (maybe 300 pounds, four feet long?) in a gully in the coral about 40 feet below. Pointing it out to us, he made a beautiful dive (I was filming with my super 8mm movie camera), coasting in slowly towards the giant. I think he actually touched it on the back. The Jewfish, in no hurry, started swimming slowly out of the gully and across the drop-off edge. We had what seemed like a long time to watch it, but probably only a bare minute. It's in my movie, now on video.

Another day in 1969, when no group was on the island, I went with Jorn out to the reef to observe and photograph huge coral heads, rising up thirty feet almost to the surface. He used me in some photos to help measure the size. When finished, he suggested we snorkel home downwind, letting the boat drift behind us, to see what the sandy flats inside the reef were like. I had never done this before, except for the day we found the giant conchs, assuming it was bare and uninteresting. But I learned from Jorn that when you calmly devote yourself to careful observation even the most desolate landscape becomes interesting, with more life than you expected.

There were numerous pyramids of sand, obviously built by some creature. There were winding tracks. Scattered outcrops of rock had seafans (beautiful Flamingo Tongue shells crawling on them) and many species of soft-coral seawhips, all requiring a solid base. An occasional stingray swam slowly along the bottom, or lay half buried in the sand, only eyes exposed. A passing nurse shark, also close to the bottom, ignored us. Here came a school of Goat Fish, stirring up a cloud of fine sand as they fed on tiny organisms. (Later, in the Bahamas, I often saw these "clouds" from small planes.) There were colorful starfish and black spiny sea urchins, all quietly feeding and reproducing in their own life styles. Finally we came to the turtle grass, extending on in the six-foot shallows almost to shore, where there was a final narrow band of sand kept clear by tides and surf. Still unknown to me, there were sea horses, and many other fascinating creatures, in the turtle grass. So, though it was not a spine-tingling adventure, it was far more interesting than I expected, another chapter in learning from the Sea.

The next day Jorn said he was going to walk to Manchioneal Hill in the SE to look for fossil coral he had heard was there, inviting me to come. We started out, making our way on small paths I had never seen, over the hills, passing scattered homes. At noon we stopped with a family who cooked us lunch. We had fun with their children. Arriving at Manchioneal Hill, Jorn almost immediately found outcrops of fossil coral, taking samples with his geological rock hammer. He gave me a piece which I treasure, with winding million-year-old worm holes, the limestone homes of each coral polyp clearly visible.

Then Jorn made an exciting find—a large embedded shell which looked like it might be a Pacific-type Tridacna—here in the Atlantic Caribbean! Jorn wrote me on July 6, 1972, that "it turned out to be an oyster of the genus Ostrea." I took this picture of Jorn holding this fascinating discovery.

Later I learned from Dr. Carter Gilbert, an ichthyologist leading another of my groups, that there are similar species of fish on both sides of the Isthmus, with distinct differences but obviously with common ancestry (from the time when the oceans were connected). Darwin would have loved that information!

I've continued to learn from Jorn. He sends me each new paper he writes, and is generous with advice and information. He is deeply concerned about worldwide ecological damage to coral reefs, mostly from mankind's ignorance and greed. He has a special love for Old Providence Island and its people. For all of us, including all the Life on the coral reefs, I want to say—thank you Jorn!

IRONWOOD HILL & AIRSTRIP

Ironwood Hill is the most prominent peninsula on Old Providence, jutting out to the east towards the Brothers Cays. When we were first there it was undeveloped and unused, except occasionally for cattle pasture. We heard that it was owned by James Rankin, a notoriously large landowner, stories going around of how he somehow obtained title when people were behind on taxes.

One spectacular day Ali and I went for a long walk up onto the ridge of Ironwood, and out to the point, a commanding view of cays and reef. We began to have fantasies of how this beautiful spot might be used—and, as our fantasies grew, we found our selves talking of buying it! We had no money, but maybe we could make a down payment and arrange a mortgage. We were told by island friends that we would probably end up losing our money, and with no title. But, we were not to be discouraged.

Ali, having grown up on the moors of Scotland had dreams of raising cattle. I knew nothing of cattle, was even afraid to walk across a pasture, even if there were only cows, no bull! I got angry at her. We had a bad scene, up there alone, with sea and clouds and trade winds—very sad.

My private fantasy was to reserve the best spot for a marine biology laboratory, the best in the Caribbean. Then there would be home sites along the shore, for islanders and ourselves, at reasonable prices. Later, the fantasy grew to include a protected park covering most of the hill. There was no ironwood left, only patchy trees, bushes, and grass. Maybe experts could study its history and try to return Ironwood Hill to what it may have been like a thousand years ago . . . exciting! Ali would have agreed, if my temper hadn't ruined our morning.

We made an offer, and, if we had persevered, it might have become a reality. But, Rankin was hesitant about price. and, gradually, we came to realize that we would rather be visitors than full time residents.

In about 1966-67 plans for an airstrip were making headway. There was a long naturally flat north-south muddy area between Ironwood and Bailey, maybe 100 meters wide. I seem to remember that when I went back alone in 1966 a plane had tried to land, unsuccessfully, and the wreck was still there.

I may have been the first, or one of the first, to take air photos of Providence. In 1966 I had heard that a cargo plane went empty from San Andres to Miami once a week. I asked the pilot if I could go with him the following week, and he said . . . "maybe . . . just show up at 6 AM." I went to San Andres on the ARCABRA, arriving after midnight. I told Capt. Ulrich I had to go ashore at dawn, and asked how I could get to the beach. He said there would be a dugout canoe by the boat, and I could just leave it on the beach. So, my day started in a dugout, then a taxi to the airport. The Capt. said OK, and yes, he would fly once around Providence. I took a roll of photos, then shivered the rest of the way to Miami even under three blankets.

I soon boarded a jet, less than half full, so the stewardess, hearing my story, gave me three lunches. That trip from Old Providence to Miami, was the most dramatic "reentry" experience of my life! From dugout canoe, to taxi, to cargo plane, to jet!

I made some recordings of rush-hour traffic on radio, to play for my groups on their last day. "Reentry", from Providence, is always a painful experience!

By 1968 there were two or three flights a week, but for years the strip was unpaved. Once, after heavy rains, when I had a group coming, the pilot grudgingly agreed to fly up to Providence and take a look, but did not guarantee to land. When we got there, the field was covered with huge ponds of water, and he said, no way, his family came first. One of my group members decided Providence was not for her, and went back home, but the next sunny day the rest of us made it. My movie has a scene of one of our members, a nurse, hamming it up as she headed the wrong way from plane to pickup truck, finding herself ankle-deep in a huge mud puddle.

For the next few years Providence had a series of little air services, sometimes lasting only months.

Now, Ironwood Hill, both islands, and the uninhabited cays, are all part of the United Nations Seaflower Biosphere Preserve . . . as it should be.

GENERAL CLEMENT DISCOVERS PROVIDENCE HUMOR

One day in the late 1960's General Clement arrived at Old Providence Island from the United States and was staying with Mr. Ray Howard (where I had a room also.)

He was chuckling over some of the new words he was learning at Providence. Mr. Ray was complaining about having to deal with a "Spanish liar." (In the islands "lawyer" is pronounced "liar".) General Clement laughed and said: "We have a lot of liars who call themselves lawyers in the United States too, but we seldom have the nerve to call them liars to their face!"

Mr. Ray said: I hear you went to visit the "mare" (island pronunciation for "mayor".) "Yes, I was trying to ask him about going through customs. Do you call it the iguana? He laughed and explained to me that customs is called "aduana" in Spanish.

Then the mayor let me ride to Southwest Bay in the town dump truck, saving me 47 pesos—about a US penny—high finance!—I already love Old Providence Island. I think maybe I'll retire here."

ALL-NIGHT-REPAIR WITH
BERTRAM

A neighbor in Bailey, Bertram Fernandez, often known as "Bandit", became one of my earliest friends among the island divers. In fact, I learned later, that he was the very first who learned to use mask-snorkel-and-flippers, taught by Bob Marx. When I needed a dependable friend to run the air compressor, he was the natural choice. It was a tough job—noisy, hot, long hours into the night after a regular day's work on the dive raft—to get all the tanks properly filled for the next day's diving. It required quite a bit of knowledge and experience, not only in running the compressor itself safely at high pressures, but also the gasoline engine which powered it.

One afternoon, near the beginning of a 10-day dive group, the compressor sprang a leak at one of the brass couplings in the high pressure tubing. It would no longer reach the required pressure. Instead of quickly filling a tank to 2000 pounds, it would only slowly go to 1000, and then would go no higher, no matter how long we kept it running. We easily located the leak by its loud hiss, but I had no spare parts. At that time there were probably no high pressure fittings even in San Andres. The closest were Panama (possibly?) or Miami—many days shipping time away. In those years we didn't even have epoxy or other cement for metal repairs.

We took it apart and carefully examined the damaged fitting. It was a miniature egg-shaped metal part with a hole through the center for the tubing. When the outer threaded coupling was tightened, the metal-to-metal surfaces compressed until it was leak-proof.

Could we make a new fitting? We would sure give it a try! We collected all the tools we could find: files, hack saws, drills, emery cloth, Vise-Grips, hammers—and went to work. It turned out to be mostly filing, all by hand. The hours went by. Our fitting began to slowly take shape.

Finally, in the wee hours of the morning, it was looking good—time to assemble, tighten everything up, and give it a try. The pressure went up to 1000, 1500 . . . no hiss . . . we stayed safely back . . . 1700 . . . 2000! Success!

Bertram went home to catch a few winks. I managed to sleep for an hour or two. All tanks were full, ready for the morning dive.

Thank you, Bertram! This was just one of many times when you didn't watch the clock, working till the job was finished.

HENRY MORGAN CAPTURES PROVIDENCE

This morning at dawn, a few stars still visible, I'm off to climb the hill above town to look for Henry Morgan's ships. Finding a steep stairway between two houses, I follow a dim path. Now above the roofs of town, I climb through tall grass, passing someone's cistern. A startled hen takes off with loud clucking to fly an amazing 200 yards down to the main street.

Even here in the Caribbean, there's a chill in the sea breeze. Dew soaks my sneakers. Water color splashes of pink and gold join sky and sea. Sunrise tints are spreading completely around the horizon, a richer glow in the east where expanding rays mount the sky, almost like an aurora. I pause to let it all soak in . . . the full glory of a new sunrise . . . mountains . . . cays . . . reefs . . . and ocean to the far horizon . . . one of Nature's most glorious spectacles!

Climbing higher, slowly turning back the calendar, houses below me disappear, one by one. Soon, even the wreck of James Rankin's schooner "Rembreau," dugout canoes and catboats . . . are gone. I sit, at last, high on a rock, feeling a tingle of excitement as I scan the horizon out past Catalina Island. It is strangely quiet, not even a rooster crowing, very unusual for Providence where roosters crow at any hour. When one starts, a chain-reaction sweeps around the island. But now there is only the perennial far off roar of surf on the reef. A brilliant ruby emerges from the sea. It is sunrise . . . 1670.

But I'm not alone on Providence Island. Spanish soldiers are sleeping, not knowing what I know, that Morgan's fleet is coming . . .

Henry Morgan is a most important part of Old Providence life. Islanders, keenly proud that this famous English buccaneer sea captain came to their island on his way to sack Panama in 1670, named a dramatic rock on the west side of Catalina, "Morgan Head". They are especially proud that he was English (because of their own English heritage), that he was a great sailor (islanders are the best sailors in Colombia), and that he defeated the Spaniards (they have little use for "Sponyards"). Some like to believe he left descendants on the island. Many think he returned from Panama, with treasure beyond imagining, to bury some of it here. Others feel this may be doubtful, for Sir Henry, knighted in Jamaica, had plenty of time, money, and opportunity to come back, if he had so chosen.

(For more on the addictive fascination of treasure, see Bob Marx and Treasure.)

So, as I sit high on the hill, my own deep love for Old Providence Island stirs many thoughts and emotions . . . surprisingly, even an unexpected tear. My friend, Morgan Bush, was one who carried on the name "Morgan."

(see A Day in the Life of a Fisherman, Morgan Bush.)

As the sun rises, its warmth is welcome. I scan the horizon. Then, movement catches my eye, far to the northwest, a sail! Now, coming into view around the west of Catalina, a ship is already close in, not more than two miles out. Under full sail, not yet in the lee of the island, still catching the trade wind. Now another, and more . . . I slowly count . . . thirty eight . . . a formidable fleet, heading in towards Southwest Bay.

I see a puff of smoke from one ship . . . then, seconds later, hear the boom of a cannon. A cloud of dust rises from the fort as a cannon is hit, and topples. That will wake up the "Sponyards"! It has sent my boyhood "pirate blood" surging.

The story goes that Morgan demanded immediate surrender, but accepted a compromise requested by the Spanish commander. Both sides would engage in a mock battle, before the overwhelming English numbers forced surrender.

I'm afraid it isn't realistic to think of Morgan as a hero to admire. Of course he was a brilliant commander and strategist, but also a buccaneer as brutal as they come. Those who wish to read more will enjoy: THE BUCCANEERS OF AMERICA, by John Esquemeling; THE SPANISH MAIN, by Philip A. Ainsworth; A GENERAL HISTORY OF THE PIRATES, by Captain Charles Johnson, first published in 1726.

As the last ship passes behind the point, suddenly roosters are crowing. Houses and boats reappear . . . it's 1966.

Reentering the real world, I start back down the hill. Early risers in town greet me, curious as to where I've been . . . (if they only knew!) "Mr. Ray" Howard, from whom I rent a room above his store, asks if I want scrambled eggs for breakfast. What taste! Eggs from free-ranging hens, freshly laid this morning, a far cry from supermarket "factory-made-eggs". As I eat I'm imagining Henry Morgan provisioning his ships for Panama: live turtles, pigs, chickens, iguana . . . oranges, bananas, water, rum . . . his men not knowing if they would ever see Jamaica, or England, again . . . "Jamaica, Farewell" . . .

VICTOR "MISTER RAY" HOWARD

Mr Ray says that after breakfast he can tell me his life story, as I had requested. I'm eager to hear it. He is one of the most respected elders of the island. My tape recorder is ready:

"Well, like I was told by my old parents, and other old relatives, no? talking about the origin of . . . our first father, grandfather who came here. I don't remember what year, but his name was Simon Howard, the first Howard to ever come to this island. He was my great grandfather. He was supposed to come from Baltimore. He was mixed with Negro and Indian. I've seen his picture. He was dark complexioned. Hair wasn't straight like a real Indian, but he had fairly straight hair, a bit curly. He was a Baptist minister.

He married my great grandmother, Anna Falda(?), from Seemotey(?), department of Bolivar, Colombia, and had several children. He also had children by another woman. He had two sons, Simon and Eusabia, who were also ministers. After he died my father,

Felix Alpheus Howard, was ordained. After he died the church had
no minister for awhile, till Silvano May came from San Andres. Then
my brother Ricalde was ordained minister. Ever since his death the
church has no real minister, just the deacons in charge. Today Mr.
Olvideo Howard is deacon in charge.

I was told that before any religion was here there was a woman
named Hosevia, she used to preach but she had no church. Before that
someone came here on a vessel and said the only sign of religion he
could see was that people rested on Sunday, the onliest kind of religion
people had here, maybe a couple of hundred years ago. I completed
69 the 21st of Dec. Born 1897.

I remember when Panama separated from Colombia (I was six)
in 1903. They sent soldiers here, the first ship I had ever seen in this
harbor. They slept under the houses.

Aury? I heard the old people talk about him and his soldiers. He
died over here. In about 1940 the Intendente, of French descent,
looked for his grave, found many, separated by bricks, his officers
with uniforms.

We had teachers from Jamaica. First school I went to was Sheridan
Archbold, then John Archbold. James Rankin attended the same
school, he was further advanced, was like a monitor, used to hear my
lessons. I figure he was a couple of years older.

I was working all my school days. My father had plantations, pigs,
cows. Before sunrise, then after school till sundown! Milking cows
from 5 in the morning. Sometimes I had to leave school and go to
work. No cisterns in those days. People had to go to Freshwater Bay
to carry water back here. I was ten when I first went to San Andres.

My father had a little store right on this spot. After he died of
stroke in 1928 I bought out from the other children, break that down
and built this house here. I married in 1926, gave up idea of going to
the US, could make out here.

Remember wreck of steamship NAVARRA, loaded with pine
lumber. I been out there and saw it. (many island homes built from
that lumber) Then a three masted schooner, DIX, always sailing from
islands to Baltimore, brought merchandise and took coconuts. And

the CRYSTEL VINNEN, steel-hulled five-masted, like a square rigger, struck the reef and a few days later sank right down.

Turtle fishing . . . used to go to the Mosquito Cays, nobody troubled them, watch in the night to turn Green turtles when they came to lay, the biggest industry in those days. They sometimes stayed two months, never took women, set long nets at channels, also peg and staff to strike them if floating, like a harpoon.

Until about 30 years ago the fishermen from Cayman used to go to Mosquito Cays and bring them here to butcher . . . trade the meat for provisions (yuka, yam, syrup), a lot of vessels came to Providence, for many years, introduced the ring net. They would butcher turtles at the cays, corn it up, always provided with good amount of salt, always plenty of meat to eat, even raw, corned turtle meat tastes good! Plenty of people just roast it on fire,

Around 1920 turtle shell was worth up to $20 American money, and that was plenty! for one pound! And sometimes one turtle had up to 100-200 pounds. The meat was just a side issue, would never sell it, just give it around to friends, but the shell was what was worth.

Remember about a dozen wrecks, most were on west or south, were able to get off by dumping cargo. Three banana wrecks, two in south and one in Quito Suena which was brought here so islanders could have bananas. The Lady Sybil, 5-masted square rigger wrecked outside reef south of rocky point, steel hull, loaded with tin, divers get big fish out there.

DIX was total loss at point-of-reef about 1913-18 full of provisions. Crew mostly islanders, all or most were saved. One of several ships which made regular runs to Baltimore. She would come loaded with provisions and supply all Providence storekeepers taking their ready cash, then to San Andres to do the same, bought coconuts with cash, back to Providence for more coconuts, then to States.

Another ship loaded with lumber hit windward reef and most of lumber came right in on island, was piled up along beach from town along shore towards Old Town. Islanders stacked it in big piles. Another was loaded with cotton seed, but islanders didn't know its value so they dumped seed and saved the bags!

Palacio is taking lead from the keel of Morning Star.

Fill by dock was done by old William Rankin, walled it with cement, had biggest house on Providence. Behind were two large warehouses, with water tanks inside collecting water off big house. Also on wharf behind were huge logs where ships were careened for cleaning. I remember Prince Frederick, over 100 tons. Rope was attached to top of mast and they would lay over on side. Old William charged a daily rate and municipality got 10%. This section was all beach before he filled for big house, was called Duppie Bay, all beach clear around to Casimiro's pig pen.

Old Town beach used to be much wider, much of it washed away in 1940 hurricane, used to have horse races there. Wally Robinson, foreman building new hotel, found three gold coins washed up there. Rankin has them. Heard of finding old graves on Old Town beach, right in sand, washed open by storms, also very large old tree stumps. When he was boy beach was about four yards further out, many coconut trees washed away, just slowly by tides. North winds also brought in fish, used to catch huge numbers of Margate in bay, but not for a long time.

Ray is positive that there was an old bridge to Catalina, channel was not dredged. There is a spot near Casimiro's pig pen which is still called "the bridge" because the bridge started there. When I was young, often saw remains of the old posts, and feels that boys could still find some. It crossed, not at shallow area to East, but at deepest part of channel, which is only twenty feet wide ? to Catalina. You can clearly see the narrow blue water of the channel.

Area right around my house, built in 1935, was formerly very low and swampy, was called Duppie swamp. After a death people often saw the Duppie walking around. Just to east of this house there used to be houses where now is water. Northwest storms made the slight changes in land level.

I remember when US President Franklin D. Roosevelt came on a cruiser, anchored within sight. He came in a small boat right to the dock here, couldn't get out because he didn't bring his crutches, but sat and talked a long time as "fellow fishermen", shook hands with me and others.

During World War II US had supply boat stationed here, seaplanes would come in to refuel, crew often came ashore. Other US ships came in for brief stops. Men came to my store for food, beer, liquor—most profitable business I ever had! Mr. Harold Kitts Milk was sent from Bogota as observer, on island for about four years, probably to see how islanders were reacting to war.

Almost entire Castro family died while out fishing, in sinking of ship by submarine. Mother went mad. One man saved himself by diving back and forth under the boat as sumarine moved around, machine gunning every person. Someone who was working in Panama heard an English-speaking person tell his wife: 'We sank a Providence Island boat today.' Other island boats were sunk because they thought they were supplying oil to Germans. These sinkings were about 1941. It was a terrible time for the islands."

One day in 1967, when the above was a long-past sad memory, an American general was visiting the island, living with Mr. Ray. He overheard us talking about a Spanish "liar", and asked me who was lieing. I explained that on the island "lawyer" is pronounced "liar". He roared with laughter. "That's pretty good! Back in the States we think that, but don't have the nerve to come right out and say it!"

With these memories, Mr. Ray lapsed into silence . . . Thank you, Mr. Ray, for sharing your life with us!

LUIS AURY

Years after Henry Morgan, another remarkable adventurer discovered Old Providence Island. As a French sea captain at the time of Napoleon's defeat, Luis Aury suddenly found himself in the far Caribbean, with a ship but "without a country".

He went to New Orleans and built quite a name for himself in the new world. I will not try to recount all his exploits, for apparently no one yet has researched his life in depth. He was Governor of Florida under Mexico, and Governor of Texas! He became a buccaneer, one who was not a pirate out for loot anywhere he could get it, but was specifically out to defeat Spain.

It is even said that he was a kind hearted man who tried to avoid killing . . . he was upper class and educated, and wrote long letters to his sister . . . but it's doubtful that he was able to avoid killing . . . ??

He discovered Santa Catalina island, what a place to make his headquarters, to fight Spain, a base once more for buccaneering. So, Aury just took Providence, apparently without firing a shot, rebuilding the fort, naming it after himself.

Having no love for Spain, he hoped to join Bolivar in his revolution. When Bolivar apparently did not quickly accept him as a comrade-in-arms, Aury decided to fight Spain on his own. He soon captured several ships, had a fleet, and his own island!

So he continued to capture Spanish ships as they passed. How much was idealism, how much lust for wealth and glory? Probably no one knows.

We do know that, amazingly, he placed advertisements in US newspapers, inviting adventurers to join him on Old Providence Island. Many did.

The harbor and the shallow grass flats of Old Town Bay, are almost always calm, protected from the NE trade winds. But when an unusual storm swept in from the NW, his ships were suddenly vulnerable to the full force of ocean waves, with no reef protection. Aury lost his entire fleet, wrecked right in the shallow bay, but, undaunted, he soon "collected" another.

However, before he could continue his dream—he died—still young, right here on Old Providence Island. The story is that he fell from his horse. Probably few islanders would admit to that. Commodores don't fall from their horses . . . but it is a very "rocky little island", with deep gullies appearing without warning. I was once on a pickup truck, going south through Rocky Point, when we approached a horseman on the right edge of the road. Startled, the horse broke into a gallop. Before the rider could regain control they plunged into a gully, tumbling onto the rocks. I was amazed that both survived. They scrambled out on their own. The rider mounted, and rode on. The pickup didn't even stop. Independence and non-interference are traditional in Old Providence.

So, Luis Aury was gone, as suddenly as he had arrived. Apparently his followers went their separate ways, none trying to take his place or follow his dream. Luis Aury, except on Old Providence Island (where a fort and a government building bear his name) is virtually unknown. His colorful life would make a dramatic movie!

Chart HO 1372 of Old Providence Island has a drawing of a house on the ridge northeast of town, commanding views both East and West. Once, on a blue-sky white-cloud afternoon, I walked up there, wondering if Aury had stood (or possibly even lived} on that spot. I found only a vacant field, but with a very dramatic view. In the tall grass, half buried, I stumbled on a rusty bedspring. My imagination wandered—had Luis Aury's home been here? Had it possibly burned, its memory forgotten?

I sat for a while, looking out across the island to the sea—pondering . . . adventurers . . . revolution . . . buccaneers . . . independence . . . The only sound was the never-ending roar of the surf on the eastern reef, just as it was when Commodore Luis Michel Aury spent his last days here.

Will you be the one to write the complete story of his amazing life?

SMUGGLING

Isolated islands are always tempting as hideouts for smugglers. Whether it was a secret slave market, a source of liquor during Prohibition, a fuel supply for submarines, or an isolated contact for cocaine smugglers . . . the big-time mafia always try to take advantage of remote islanders.

Sadly, writers too often take advantage of the "mystery" to play up "exciting adventure", not facing the realities of "personal tragedy". In real life, I'm afraid smuggling never leads to happiness.

Two people I knew personally found only personal tragedy through this temptation.

One was my flight instructor at Danbury, CT. Just after I got my private pilot's licence, I met him on a street corner. He was very excited, boasting that he had a wonderful new job, so he and his bride were buying a house. A few days later I read in the newspaper that he was killed at 2 AM when his plane hit a power line in Florida, trying to fly in low under the radar . . . with a load of marijuana from the Bahamas . . . which would have further hurt the lives of unknown thousands of inexperienced young people.

The next week I saw his young wife, looking the other way when I passed her on the street. She lost her young husband, their new house, ending up in debt, suffering with guilt. I have heard that young pilots are often approached by agents of the drug mafia, so this sad story is only one of many.

The other was a young man in Providence. We knew four generations of his family. He was a friendly nice guy, with a future wide open to unlimited opportunity. One day two American pilots came to the island, offered him a get-rich-quick temptation. He was caught smuggling cocaine, ended in jail, bringing sadness to all his family and relatives . . . four generations.

When I was in Providence in 1999 there was a boat in the harbor with the two biggest outboard motors I've ever seen . . . probably not used for fishing.

I guess there are a whole world of far better opportunities . . . than smuggling.

WALKING ALL THE WAY AROUND THE ISLAND

Always a moving and memorable experience, on return trips to Providence, was walking with my diving buddy, Bertram Fernandez, to visit old friends around the island.

Starting south from town in early morning, we enjoy shade from the mountains going down the west side, and again coming up the east side in the afternoon. If you try it, counter clockwise is the way to go.

Bertram knows everyone, so, as we start towards Old Town, he shares recent island news and asks about the outside world. "Mr. Sid, is it really true that men have landed on the moon?" We talk about rockets, orbiting, and landing. "Now I understand."

I wave to Winston Jay's boys playing in the shallows with dugout canoes their father made just for them. Winston and his brother, Gimston (of Chinese ancestry) made Providence their permanent home years ago, becoming respected elders. For one of my groups, we rented Winston's house and often his horses. (recorded life story here)

We talk with Dr. Oswaldo Connolly at his home office, for many years the only doctor on the island. It brought memories of walking there with a high fever, for a penicillin shot. There was little other medical treatment available in those days. (recorded life story)

It's a pleasant walk down the beach to Old Town to visit Miss Gladys, widow of Nicholas Newball (known by friends as "Captain Chung"). In 1967 he sold us two plots of land on the west shore of Catalina, where we started building a foundation. Also, with our children, we lived on the second floor of a house they owned across the street from their big house. In the yard were piglets, a cold water shower, an earth-covered pit for making charcoal, chickens, mango and lime trees. The outhouse was on a wooden pier at the beach a hundred yards away. We swam with neighborhood children beside fishing boats. In nearby sand were pieces of hand blown bottles, air bubbles in the glass, some possibly dating from the Puritan colony. We were part of a fishing village, a great place for children.

Cattle were driven to pasture in the morning, and back home past our fence in the evening. Still inexperienced, we let our daughter, Bryn, play by the fence one evening, when suddenly the cattle came home, on the trot. One lowered its head and butted Bryn safely out of the way into the grassy ditch. Thank you, friend cow!

When my groups were on the island, Miss Gladys supplied us each day with a huge pot of her wonderful cooking. We picked it up by outboard motor boat just before mealtime.

As Bertram and I approached, Miss Gladys was sitting on the porch. We talked of her children, Betty, Edburn (who returned as a teacher), and Nicholas, and of the wonderful times our family had with her. She once told Ali, in a conversation about women riding, she used to visit friends on horseback, but no longer. On my last trip, sadly, she was very ill, in San Andres, too sick to visit. We have happy memories of you, Miss Gladys! Nearby was the little home of Alvaro Garcia, another expert diver who worked with my groups. One day, when we first met, I heard that he was seriously stung across his chest and shoulder by a large Portuguese Man of War, one of the most dangerous creatures for divers. Alvaro was not afraid of sharks but, after this encounter, was carried home screaming. He could hardly breath. I visited him the next day and took this picture, which was published in a book along with another photo of my friend Bob Straughan who had a similar near-tragedy.* Bob was snorkeling alone in Biscayne Bay near Miami, collecting salt water aquarium fish. A passing fisherman, seeing him wildly waving, thought he was a madman and hesitated to stop, but finally took him to the hospital.

Look out for Portuguese Men of War. Their stinging tentacles hang like thorny threads (a few inches or even to 33 feet) below the iridescent bluish purple float with which they sail slowly in the breeze. Unfortunate fish which touch one will be stunned, pulled up, and digested. Amazingly, the Man-of-war Fish swims carefully among the tentacles eating scraps. However, if it is forced against the stinging nematocysts, it will die.* Even a few broken threads, on the sand or an anchor line, give a nasty sting and send many swimmers to the hospital. (Alvaro's recording)

Just a few houses up the road from Miss Gladys lived Bunny and Flornesta, a special friend of Ali's when we were neighbors. Bunny was a carpenter-preacher, a remarkable person, reminiscent of the Carpenter of Nazareth. One day I heard the tragic news that their young son had just died. I walked sadly up the road to visit, finding a group of friends and neighbors, quietly talking. Bunny was in the front yard, making a coffin. It was not just a box, but beautifully crafted, wider at the shoulders, tapering at head and feet, to fit the small body.

As he worked, Bunny talked of their family, the joys—and tragedies. He was carefully sanding the edges smooth. Quietly he told the story of each child, living and dead. Their friends also remembered happy and sad times they had together. It was a community of shared experience. There was no ceremony or exaggerated polite words. It was a mutual sharing, a struggle to accept life's mysteries. It was the most natural way for a community to share the tragic mystery of death that I've ever seen.

This time Bertram had told me the almost unbelievably sad news that Bunny had very recently died. As we approached the house, Flornesta (maybe seeing us coming) was standing in the road by her gate, tears in her eyes. I gave her a quiet hug, saying that Bunny had changed our lives. As we quietly walked on, there were tears in my eyes.

On my most recent visit Flornesta told me she has been raising someone else's child. Not many children without a family are so lucky. Bunny would be happy.

At the end of Old Town beach we climbed the peninsula called Camp, and north on a side trail to visit Mr. Jonathan Archbold, living alone in a little shack, above his home where his second wife and daughters lived. A magnificent giant mango tree, probably the largest on the island, towers over their house. We found Mr. Jonathan alone in his shack. His family brought him food, but he often cooked for himself. The story was that one day he left his first wife and family on Catalina, and moved across the bay to start a new life.

We knew his son Oswero and wife Olivia, grandchildren Oswero, Willesley, Eloisa and her husband Carol Robinson, postman; great grandchildren (the Robinson family) two sons tragically lost at sea, Eleoma, Richard, and Aminta (now manager of the supermarket)—four generations! Willesley once was approached by a visiting pilot, yielded to the temptation of cocaine smuggling, was caught and jailed. Everyone suffered. But, probably, people around the world (and especially in the U.S.) are most responsible—by creating a market for cocaine and permitting it to continue.

We sat down with Mr. Jonathan, looking out at Catalina and the spreading horizon of the sea, and talked for a long time. Till recently, he was able to put on his best clothes, stand on a box to mount, and ride into town to visit, a grand old man on horseback, not to be forgotten. Now, he was a hermit, land-rich but penny-poor, enjoying his magnificent property and ocean view—alone.

Mr. Jonathan is no longer with us. There was no one else like him, or ever will be. Thank you, Mr. Jonathan, for all we learned from you, and even for the unanswered questions . . .

As we regained the main road, we saw Father Martin walking toward us. We have known his brother, Ronald Taylor and family, very well for many years, but, sadly, have not seen Father Martin as often. Their mother, was one of the most remarkable elder women of the island. I especially appreciated the time when he invited my group to a dance program at the Catholic church in Lazy Hill when a dancer from Colombia was studying the traditional island English dances, and a group of young people performed. Father Martin has shared with us a bit of his life story:(add)

Leaving Lazy Hill we came to Freshwater Bay, an attractive small beach which was becoming a tourist center—perfect timing for lunch on the beach with a friend of Bertram's.

Then a long walk around the rocks above Bat Hole, down the horse racing beach of Southwest Bay, and over the ridge near the lighthouse. Suddenly we hear the roar of surf as the eastern barrier reef comes in sight. The main road bypasses Manchioneel Bay, a beautiful secluded beach where no one lived.

We stop to visit Rev. and Mrs. Rudolph Newball, who did so much to develop the Adventist schools. Their boys, going too far out in a dugout one day, drifted to Nicaragua. Lynd became a doctor in San Andres, married a marine biologist. One day as I was walking down the sidewalk by the San Andres beach, an attractive young woman came up beside me on a motor scooter: "I'm here to pick you up. Hop on." Before my ego had a chance to get too inflated, she explained that she was Dr. Newball's nurse. He had seen me out the window, and sent her to bring me for a visit.

Captain Ulric's house is nearby, and, luckily, he's home. I see his powerful HAM radio for the first time, dozens of call-letter cards on the wall from friends around the world he has talked with. I bring him one of my photos of the ARCABRA being loaded with oranges and cattle. (life story recording)

Not far north we find Amanda's house, and she is there with her two boys. She was twelve on our first trip, and took care of Bryn while we snorkeled. On my last visit she was a nurse in San Andres.

Arriving at Bertram's home right beside the airstrip, Alihandrina had cooked a wonderful soup for us. I record them singing hymns as they do in church, then take photos of nine family members at home (one son at work and another in California). I admire their banana and papaya trees, and Bertram's brand new lawn mower. A grand daughter hugs me: "It's the man with the camera!" She loved to see the camcorder's instant replay.

Continuing towards town, we cross the street to visit Joe Ward and family: "my last", he informs me. He looks great. He, also, is now proudly a church member. Years ago he was usually seen operating heavy construction equipment, had built most of the island roads, as well as being well known as the proud father of twenty-five children. I recorded his life story in 1968.

And there is Miss Bacola whose sugar cookies, so wonderfully baked over charcoal, warmed the hearts of my family and groups. And here is her son, Kelly, Frank Reed's freezer plant manager and boat captain. We talk of old times.

Coming into town, I visit Ronald Taylor and Alvaro Howard across the street, who have helped us over the years in too many ways to count.

Reaching town, we find Miss Bress, retired nurse, playing dominoes with three friends. I told her how I remembered the wonderful taste of her homemade ice cream. People walked miles to town to buy it, because it was the only ice cream on Providence. She smiles: "I still make it!" Miss Bress, also, has shared her life story:

One night which Ali, being a mother, remembers even more vividly than I, we were on the pickup coming home with the kids from a horse race at Southwest Bay, when we stopped in front of a house. The driver said we would wait to take Miss Bress home, as soon as she finished delivering a baby. We could hear her talking to the mother. Occasionally a pan of water was thrown out the window. The prospective father, and neighbors, came over to chat with us. It was a quiet night, except for crickets and the Providence "bubbling" frogs . . . Then came the baby's cry. Another new adventurer had burst into the open air of Old Providence Island. There were many others being born around the world that night, about three every second, but for us this one was very special.

Miss Bress was soon climbing into the pickup. Ali asked her if it was an easy birth. She smiled: "Of course." Recently I asked her to estimate how many babies she has delivered. "Many." For all of them, all of us, I can only say, thank you, Miss Bress!

On the street I luckily find Rodrigo Howard, science teacher, who has land on Catalina between ours and the fort beach.

We stop at Willie B's home where he and his group put on a mini-concert just for me to record. His mandolin, and songs written in Providence, bring memories to both of us of great parties over the years, and of the coral reefs:

"Uncle Bug is under the reef . . . " (island song)

It's getting dark, so I say goodnight to Bertram and continue across the bridge to my room on Catalina. Memories flood in, of Bertram, my best friend on Providence—thank you—for all the wonderful experiences we have shared over so many years!

BLUE HOLE, CHANNEL MOUTH, FAVORITE DIVE SPOTS

Old Providence Island offers many spectacular dive spots, and, undoubtedly, many more undiscovered. Here are a few of our favorites. I am not the only one who rates Old Providence more beautiful than the Bahamas. Ben Rose, a Bahamian with unmatched diving experience, was one of our group leaders. He quickly acknowledged that Old Providence had more dramatic coral, more variety, more sharks, all in all, more exciting diving. I noticed recently that Ben was among worldwide divers with over 5000 hours experience. Also included were several other members and leaders of Adventures in Marine Biology . . . Eugenie Clark, Stan Waterman, Paul Tzimoulis, and Hardy Jones.

"Blue Hole" has a special meaning in Providence. Rather than a deep circular cave formed by water when the seas were lower (as in Bahamas, Belize, and Yucatan) in Old Providence it is a drop-off edge, where the coral formations at about 30 feet, drop off vertically to 100 feet and more. There is a spectacular variety of coral here, with the central section at about 50-70 foot depth possibly the most dramatic.

For safety, we made no scuba dives over 100 feet, so required no decompression stops before surfacing. We never had an accident. All members were required to have graduated from an accredited course, and have an official certificate. Sadly, the few exceptions were the marine biologists themselves, and their wives! Once, when I was not present, I was told that several divers went deeper than 100 feet. The wife of our leader came to the surface almost unconscious, disoriented. She was quickly towed to the boat by one of our island divers.

I was also very strict about requiring each diver to stay oriented during their scuba dive, so they could always surface beside the boat. One girl showed her inexperience, when she surfaced 100 yards away and tried to swim toward the boat with tank still on her back, and no snorkel. When she began to flounder, I glanced at one of the island divers who was there in a flash and towed her back. An experienced scuba diver will always have snorkel attached to mask. Surfacing, they will take their tank off, and snorkel with the tank under their chest so that it gives some buoyancy rather than weighting them down. In those days we did not yet use buoyancy regulators, though inflatable life jackets were required.

Another day at Blue Hole I was at about 50-feet when I saw my island friend Bertram coming down with scuba, proudly waving at me. One of our members had very unwisely loaned his tank to Bertram. From then on I made a strong point of explaining that this was taboo. The island divers were expert free divers, but had no scuba training. Their habitual way of diving was to hold their breath when returning to the surface rapidly. For a scuba diver this of course can lead to the bends, or could be fatal. The closest decompression chamber was the U.S. Navy in Panama. I had their phone number, and trusted that they would send a plane in emergency, but I wanted to make sure that never happened. It never did. However, my greatest guilt feeling is that I did not instruct the island divers enough as to the dangers of scuba diving. It is deceptively easy, but, without training, can kill you. I will discuss this more in a later chapter, "Providence Today".

Not only the coral, but also the fish are especially numerous at Blue Hole. A large school of Spadefish, drifting parallel to the dropoff, is unforgettable. Large grouper are numerous. Sharks and Barracuda are seldom seen here, probably because they like to hunt closer to the surf where oxygen is richer. Angel fish of all types can be easily approached.

Another interesting spot is known as "Channel Mouth". When the seas were lower, one of the island's streams flowed out towards the NW, carving a channel about 100 feet wide, which now drops from about 30 feet to a 60-foot sand bottom where Garden Eels are numerous. These tiny eels extend about eight inches from their burrow, facing the current, so they can swallow plankton as it drifts by. When a diver approaches, they of course disappear into the sand. With modern camcorders it would be easy to place the camera close, leaving it running, while the diver backs off . . . to get an ultra-close-up of garden eels feeding . . . a challenge to you!

I read recently that undersea archaeologists are now searching the banks of these ancient river channels as possible sites of prehistoric villages. At Channel Mouth any such remains would probably be buried in the sand.

At numerous places along the eastern barrier reef (such as just northeast of Crab Cay) there are dramatic narrow channels through the reef. With sand bottoms, the walls rise vertically 20 or 30 feet. There is usually too much surf at the surface to snorkel through, but with scuba you can wind your way along the bottom, and soon find yourself in dramatically deeper and clearer water, outside the reef, sometimes with three sharks visible at once. One of our members, at lunch after one such dive, said: "I don't know if it was Heaven or Hell, but I'll never forget it!"

Further north is a wonderful place which we named "The Blue Spot." From the air, there is a noticeable blue sandy area where it was easy to anchor in calm water just inside the reef. At the reef itself there was a large protected "cave" which seemed always to be filled with thousands of circling fish. Snorkeling through to the outside, the depth dropped to 40-50 feet, clarity noticeably better, maybe 200 feet? It was fairly calm, as there were more coral heads further out. As in the Gulf Stream near Bimini, divers experience a strange "magnifying" effect from one's mask, a little unnerving.

We seldom used scuba here because to snorkel out and back was a lifetime experience. I took Ali's sister, Marj, in '71. Even though she was not an experienced snorkeler, she seemed to be handling herself well, and wanted to go. I told the island divers to keep an eye on us, as we snorkeled slowly out, 100 yards, and back. I also took

Mrs. Betsy Lawrence in '69. In a few short minutes she saw her first three sharks.

I have already told about Lawrence Reef, where Ali and I saw the giant Barracuda. It is a beautiful place, close to town. Another shallow reef, a mile further north is known as Catalina Bar, hard to beat for watching and photographing small fish. I used to challenge our members to practice observing, carefully. It is easy for an amateur to imagine that the fish are "just swimming around" at random, but are they? Pick one, and watch it carefully. How far does it go, and what is it doing? Is it feeding? Guarding its territory? Are there some fish which come from a distance, and travel on far down the reef, while others may stay within a few feet of one spot? Can you find a cleaning station? Before "cleaning stations" were known, we of course often saw a big grouper poised in one spot with its mouth slightly open. But we didn't observe carefully enough. We didn't notice the cleaner fish. If we had just observed more carefully we could have written the first paper about cleaning stations.

Occasionally we made a night dive in the shallows near Morgan Head, though this was a fairly new experience in those years. The first thing we always noticed was many octopus, out in the open, seldom seen in the daytime. We could come close, to watch them in detail. Occasionally we would find a sleeping Parrot Fish, in it filmy "coocoon-nightshirt" which it exudes to protect itself. Especially interesting were the basket starfish, which extend themselves like a net at night, their dozens of tiny arms straining the passing current for plankton. We kept an eye out for passing sharks, but never saw one.

The shallows around Bat Hole on the NW side of Catalina were a favorite beginning dive. It gave me a chance to see how the divers handled themselves. I always challenged them to never touch the coral, certainly never to stand on it or try to hold on. I challenged them by saying that an experienced snorkeler never gets in a vertical position, or takes off their mask to get the water out. An experienced snorkeler always remains horizontal, never holds onto anything, but drifts with the current. Of course, an experienced snorkeler is expert at rolling on their side or back to expel a little water from their mask (but should have fitted their mask so carefully that it would not leak.) The first dive, out on the reef, is NOT the time to be fiddling with mask-strap-adjustment. That should be done in a pool before leaving home. To test a mask, put it on your face wet, without using the strap, then inhale slightly through your nose. Your mask should stay firmly on your face as long as you can hold your breath. If it falls off, you need a different mask.

But, there was sometimes a snorkeler (like the marine biologist's wife) to be seen standing on the coral, weaving back and forth in the current, later complaining about scratches, and not being able to sleep because of coral burns.

Some unusually beautiful fish, such as High Hats, were seen especially often here. The visibility was only fair, so I tried to plan dives to be progressively better.

Another beginners spot was White Shoal, with nice shallow coral surrounded by a mini-barrier-reef, in calm water.

Bertram first took me to Newball Reef, a dramatic area. It is necessary to cross over some very shallow coral to get there. In clear-water depths of 30 feet grow the most magnificent elkhorn coral I've ever seen, dwarfing those in the Bahamas where Twenty Thousand Leagues Under the Sea was filmed.

Bertram shouted to me, pointing down. There was one of the biggest sharks I had ever seen, maybe over eight feet, with a very solid body. Macho Bertram dove and bounced a spear off of this giant, which swam away in a hurry.

Though it is seldom calm enough to go easily outside the East reef, a top favorite dive was the wreck of the Chrystal Vinnen, a huge steel-hulled square rigger, owned by the German Vinnen Line. With a cargo of nitrates (bags of bird guano) it had appeared one day outside the reef, drifting in, to finally wreck—some feel on purpose. It was certainly not a storm. On my first visit, the long bowsprit was still at the surface. One huge anchor, still at the bow. The wreckage is strewn over a large area, steel beams giving an accurate measurement of growth rate for brain coral, sea fans, seawhips, and other life forms, since the exact date of the wreck is known.

In 1978 there was a new wreck outside the eastern reef, a freighter, the "LISA", about 4 miles north of the Crystal Vinnen, about five miles east and slightly north of town. It had already been stripped of all valuables when we went there with Bryn and Craig, ages 12 and 14. It was far out and fairly deep, so was a bit scary for them. On the way back Craig caught a Barracuda, which made his day.

There are other wrecks undiscovered, and, of course, there will be more in the future.

THE FORT

Over the centuries since the Puritan colony, the fort has been built and rebuilt many times. In Jan. of 1965 I had to spend half an hour cutting grass before I could take a photo of the cannon, but when I returned in 1967 much of the area had been cleared by the municipality, the cannons clearly visible from the sea. Those who brave the thorns to explore in detail are amazed at how much human labor has gone into reshaping that hill! Great moats were chiseled into solid rock. Intricate cement work is sometimes hard to distinguish from the natural volcanic conglomerate. Cannon balls were so numerous in the bushes and shallows that visitors found them easily, only to have them taken by the government, and themselves put on the next boat.

Today when you come to Providence, few ever go up to the fort. It is just a sad quiet reminder of a violent past, almost lost in the beautiful green hills of Catalina.

MORGAN BUSH—A DAY IN THE LIFE OF A FISHERMAN

It was a very special privilege to get to know Morgan Bush, fisherman-philosopher. He had inherited, and learned from his own life-experience, a vast understanding of Nature. You couldn't spend an hour with him without getting fascinating new insights. I learned from him that fishing in itself can be an art. One day I asked him if I could go along with him for a day of fishing, and take pictures. He welcomed me, so the next morning—early—I met him at his home on Catalina.

First he threw his net in the shallows for "sprat" (bait fish.) Then we were off, he and his buddy, Angel Webster, in a sailing catboat, I following in my outboard. It was a gorgeous day.

The catboat is an amazingly beautiful design. The more you learn about it, the more impressed you become. Basicly it is a dugout, with gunwale planks added to complete the hull, coming to a point fore and aft. Inside it is very smooth, with a sheet of copper tacked on at the lowpoint, so it can easily be bailed with a half-gourd, water shooting out as if from a powerful bilge pump!

The mast is easily lifted from a close-fitting socket, so that the boom can be folded beside it and the sail rolled up around them, in a minute. The single sail at that time was made from flour sacks, though a few lucky ones had sailcloth salvaged from the MORNINGSTAR. As I remember, it had two seats and was steered with a paddle, Usually sailed by two, it could easily carry a passenger or two.

Islanders made ocean voyages in catboats, up to the uninhabited banks (Quito Sueno, Roncador, Serrana) to fish, harvest bird's eggs, and catch turtles (though they usually used larger boats for turtles), coming back loaded. In many ways catboats were safer than power boats, which are helpless if motor fails, and can sink. If a catboat capsizes in a storm, it can easily be righted and bailed. It can't sink.

When fishermen returned from the north, their family would sometimes put a lantern on the hilltop above town, to guide them home. I never saw a compass in a catboat, so assume they navigated by the sun and stars.

I had told Morgan that I would like to dive and take a picture looking up at him as he looked down at me through his glassbottomed bucket, so we soon stopped in the calm waters on the west side of Catalina, and I got my picture. Morgan, being a traditional island fisherman, did not dive. When I surfaced, he grinned with obvious envy: "I wish I could do that!"

We continued north to the first fishing spot, trolling on the way. They soon caught a Barracuda, holding it up for me to see. When they stopped, looking down at the coral through their glass, paddling around a bit till they found a good spot, they dropped anchor.

I came alongside to watch them bait their hooks, an art based on years of experience. Sprat were threaded on so that the hooks were hardly visible. No bait would be wasted by too easily coming off. The baited hook looked much like a swimming fish! After catching a beautiful grouper, they decided to head further north to another reef. Very suddenly, a squall swept down on us (to be expected anytime in Providence). In minutes, we were in a mini-storm, dark clouds, downpour, whitecaps, chilly wind blowing a gale! Morgan and Angel had their hands full sailing, healed way over, bailing. I had my hands full racing parallel, spray drenching me, trying to get pictures of them with my waterproof camera.

Just as quickly, the squall passed—blue sky and sunshine. Whitecaps vanished. It was warm again!

They soon caught another grouper, and we were off to town. Fishermen, knowing their market, tend to catch a little less than needed rather than too much, having no waste. On an island without refrigerators, families lived carefully from day to day, buying the minimum to avoid spoilage. I guess another advantage is that housewives who miss out, will come earlier the next day. With customers waiting, he can sell everything in a short time. Reaching town, coming alongside a rock wall in shallow water, standing thigh-deep, they cleaned the fish, discarded scraps quickly eaten by small hungry sprat below. I never saw them clean fish in the boat, thus avoiding unnecessary cleanup.

It was a successful day for Morgan and Angel, a lifetime experience for me, sharing a day in the life of a fisherman.

Some of his insights linger in my mind: August and September are often calm. Sometimes there is not a cloud in the sky, not a breath of wind. You can go anywhere on the reef. April, from middle of March, can also be calm.

"Devil Fish" (manta rays) come in these months, possibly to breed, sometimes can see a dozen out in harbor. Does not believe they ever catch an anchor rope on purpose. Has seen them swim back and forth under his anchored boat. "They never molest a boat."

Nurse sharks will bite, has seen them up to 15 feet. Sucker fish often hang onto his boat and go after bits of bait. They also cling to other big fish, Bara, etc., not only on sharks.

Some "rocks" (coral heads) out near reef north of Crab Cay are just like tables, a central post and then they spread out near surface, dark underneath. Outside the reef there are patches of pure white sand with coral heads all around.

He is the only "Morgan" on the island, had three children, but two died, four grandchildren.

Morgan Bush is no longer with us, but his children and grandchildren will have far richer lives because of all he shared with them. For me, he was one of the very most special people on Old Providence Island.

Thank you, Morgan Bush!

MR. WINSTON JAY 1/18/67

(talking about the Granja, government experimental farm)

"House built about 4 years ago, had a German there before, but did nothing, had only a shed, house started in Jan. 1963.

Used to have four laborers, but now only two, can't do nothing, have five acres, pigs, grass. Little did I know about farming, I told him we should have fertilizer and plowing. In dry weather, you don't believe it, this soil it burst and you drop down in the hole in dry weather. When the German was here take a bulldozer and push all the good soil away.

Had 500 Leghorn chickens before, but give them to school restaurant to eat. They start now with 50 of these New Hampshire, and the pigs we give out to the people, and they keep half of the increase. Also change breed, bring a common island pig and get a full breed. Sometimes find 4-5 sow in here from right around the island. Also change eggs. Sometimes have dinner for farmers here., kill hog, government gives 2000 pesos. Supposed to bring animals and produce for prizes, but never came up. People are not so interested here, need someone to teach them about agriculture. Have two diseases of coconut trees, some have hardly any nuts now, need expert to teach. I remember when they had 100 oringe trees right on this same spot here, but they all die out from the sickness. Granja should be moved to better land. This spot may be sold for highschool.

That is my land up there. Most of my time I was on the sea. When my father leave from China, he come out a young boy to Jamaica, he was 18, then he went to Panama and work as cook, you know? One of his brothers was living here in Providence so he finally came over. Brother came about 1903, had a big store here, in Bottom House. Brother got sick, went back to Panama, and to China. Then father built store in Rocky Point, sold and built store in town. He had two ships, one by name of BIRD, at first had captain Lem Newball, then afterward Marshall Archbold. Last captain was Eloseo Hawkins.

Then he bought the MIRO V, had both at same time, but I was handling the MIRO V. I was young, around 17 years, but I was handling that boat. Had motor and sail, but the BIRD was just sail. My sight was going bad on me, I quit school and go to sea. no? He also had partnership in the next boat, ENVOY, then sold his half and bought MIRO V. We were making the run to Cartegena, running the government mail, oringe, coconuts . . . two trips a month. Take oringe from here, bring general merchandise from Cartegena. Used to buy Hawksbill shell, ship it out. Used to import good from States right here, come through Christobal, Panama. I fish for scale fish but never for Hawksbill. My brother is pretty good at that, about the best around here. I fish for a big company in Bogota, had two boats, had 42 ton of Snapper fish on that boat. Came in here, and her freezer went bad, then her main motor went bad. We leave from here, towed her to Colon, a Spain captain, get down there and had to go outside the breakwater and dump 42 ton of Snapper fish overboard . . . then they change their business around . . . that was about 12-13 years ago. Those company give up and then another ship came in from Barranquilla, COMMISAR, had five ships. I used to buy fish for them. Men went out in the morning early, come back around 12-1, next fellow go out in the evening, back around 10-12 o'clock in the night, so we had a lot of work. I take care of all of that. Would take sometimes 25-40 canoes to Cays, two men in each boat, stay 5-7 days, all fishing line, no spear-gun in those days.

Two years after, Alicastro came in with his little iron hull boat, the one you see mash on the beach in Old Town, she went out and stay, the fishermen stay around. She had a very good freezer, better than COMMISAR, and we always take the fish from the fishermen there, and the COMMISAR, go to Barranquilla, and back, no? We had 75-80 men all the time out there. We got a lot of fish, in three days we can load her, 15-18 tons. But before that the German people used to fish around here. Capt. Eleseo used to fish with them. He had plenty of information about the German fishing boat. He was captain of the COMMISAR of the Cays there.

Capt. Antonio Bryan, he was captain of the CARMEN, he was fishing also when we get wreck down there . . . her refrigeration motor went bad with us. Capt. Eleseo used to work for my father, on both boats, but he has too much weight now, over 300 pounds, for several months now he can't get out.

My father give up his business, his granddaughter have a little business there. He has a daughter in Colon, visiting there now. Had five children, but a lot of grandchildren, I guess you would have to take two book to check them up! Grandchildren and great grandchildren, we have a lot of them, about 70-odd. My younger brother have about 14 children, no? I have nine. The other brother up there have 7, in front of the INA. He was engineer and then took up fishining. Price of Hawksbill is coming back, you couldn't get 50 cents a pound once, but it went up .60, .75, $1.00 keep going right up. Right here get about 40-45 pesos a pound (about $3.00).

The trouble here now there is no boat. You see that little boat they are trying to take off the beach now, they repair the motor, trying to get her seaworthy to start fishing again." (end of tape)

Thank you Mr. Winston for giving us a glimpse of the tremendous work and danger of fishing at the Cays. I hope your great grandchildren and many other readers, will enjoy this picture of your life in the early 1900's . . . truly remarkable! Thank you.

DR. OSWALDO CONOLLY

"My father, first of all, he was born in Grand Cayman, and he came over here quite a small boy, no? It happen he have some relatives over here, own a piece of land. His uncle wasn't really a turtle fisher, he had a vessel . . . he was a builder, used to build boats . . . went back to Caymons, studied navigation, came back captain of a vessel, quite young. His father was a captain too, no? Got married and live his whole life over here, got naturalized Colombian, used to run up and down Honduras, Colon, San Andres, all sail, no? Took up the run to Cartegena, oringes, mangoes from here, to Costa Rica, Puerto Limon, Colon. Coconuts, pigs, chickens. After awhile had his own ship, name of PACIT, built right here of Providence timbers, around 26 tons, 35-40 feet. It was a jigger rig, one big sail and one small, crew of around 4. Sell that and bought a bigger one, a schooner rig, name the HALCON, sailing the same run, then he lost that one. She spring a leak and went down just about 6-7 miles from San Andres, going from Providence. Still went to sea, but not on a boat of his own, no? Made quite a few trips on the VICTORIA, a steamboat from Caymons, used to take the mail from Caymons to Jamaica, then Capt. James Howard from here bought her.

I went to Cartegena to school, primary school here in Providence, and after that I study medicine, been practicing over here ever since. As a boy I made many trips with my father. When he lost his boat I was aboard at the time. In two hours time we got back to San Andres . . . there was no storm.

During the days I was studying I had quite an experience on the way to Cartegena, no? 1945, we leave here on Saturday on the sloop ENVOY, and on Monday night we came into a collision with an American boat, Coast Guard. Well, it sunk the boat. They turn back and ask us, it was dark in the night, no? ask us if we are all right. The captain answer, "No." It was blowing hard and they never heard us, no? They just leave us, and the boat went down. Was ten of us on board, on the sea in two small boats from Tuesday till Saturday. Anyway we got to the upper coast of Panama, near San Blas, quite a few days with no food or water. Went down very fast, we had time to save nothing absolutely! Extra fast. Most think it was done on purpose, but I guess, maybe, the night so dark, they never see us, no? And during the war the boats used to go without lights, no? American Lt. in charge of interrogation told captain he was to get a lawyer, no? I don't know if he ever got a lawyer, but they never got nothing.

(So you've been in two shipwrecks!)

Yes, two shipwrecks (laughing)

(Some say Providence schools were better 30-40 years ago)

Well, it could be. I'll tell you this. My grandfather from my mother's side, his name was Eucol ? Archbold, went to Cartegena for one year, came back he was mayor, was Alcalde here for several years, form a school. All those he taught were well educated, have occupied high positions after that. One of them right now is Mr. Cayatana Newball, Police Inspector in Bottom House right now. He was one of the first who started teaching Spanish. And his brother, John Archbold, my grand-uncle, was in Bogota and Alcalde here, had no more school than my grandfather teach him, no? I don't know if it was better, but it was very good. They used to teach more English in those days.

Well, progress usually brings good things and bad things (laughing). Having the experience of San Andres I believe we of this island will take better care. Yes, prices will go up and the poor people will suffer, I'm sure of that.

Have measles, chicken pox, whooping cough . . . come for a little while and then go. Once we had plenty of Malaria a few years back, but now maybe one or two cases among the old.

Nobody is really starving, but there are plenty who are not getting the right food, not sufficient protein, not enough vegetables and all those things that are necessary . . . We don't have means of getting it here, no body grow it here.

At Sanidad, they plan to put there a maternity ward, also a surgical room. At present I deliver only those that the midwives can't handle. In general island mothers have easy labor. Many babies bottle fed because they think it is modern, even though they have milk and mother's milk is best.

During the week just passed we had plenty of gripps, you know, influenza. That generally is present this time of year because of change in climate. And plenty of case of anemia . . . much need for better nutrition. Plenty could be grown here, but need somebody to instruct, because the farmers here have the old system. The earth is needing plenty of chemical (or compost).

(notice many young men with front teeth missing) Not having any dentist, when they have trouble the first thing they are thinking is to take it out, no?" (I notice also they too often use their teeth as a tool, even to take off bottle caps!)

My thoughts went back to a late night when our second baby, Craig, had trouble breathing. I ran to Dr. Connoly's house from Old Town. He came, in the middle of the night, with some camphor. Craig started breathing normally.

Thank you, Dr. Conolly, for all those years when you were the only doctor on Old Providence Island!

CAPTAINS

On Jan. 18, 1967 I visited Captain Eloseo Hawkins with my tape recorder. Here is the story of his life, in his own words:

"Born right here. Father used to go to sea, but wasn't a sea captain. Well, from what I heard, the first was old Sargent Hawkins . . . they all spring from there . . . from Morgan time.

I built this house here in 1931. My father used to live here before, but he remove and went down by the beach.

First went to sea at 17, have 52 years at sea. First ship was the ISABEL, a little ship built right here in Providence, owned by Howard, built with Providence timbers, still plenty on island in some spots to Colon. Then I sign on with Capt. Whitacker, a Caymons captain, on the VICTORY. Then I leave and went to Panama and work on the Panama Canal, on dredges . . . leave from there on a 5-mast schooner, the AMISFERRA, to United States, to New York, leave her and take a next boat, the AMY BETERVIEW, went to Haiti carry coal, and from there to Tampa, Florida. I've been running in and out from there . . . that was my home port.

Then I started work on a schooner, LADY MARION, about three years, then I gone on sister ship from her, the LAWRENCE HARVEY, between Tampa and Cuba, carry mango. Sometime we go to Honduras, Roatan . . . gone from Providence 13 years and 7 months, then I come back here 1924, things much cheaper then—turtle, fishining, and oringe was always Providence business. Grow plenty more oringe then, some years ship up to a million and a half oringes! And make up to six trips a year, that was one boat, and several boats running. First car on island about 1938, only one, own by Jay Pong . . . around '34-'38.

I never stop off the sea until about four years ago, '63 I think. From 1924 just going backward and forward. Shipwreck? Twice. But not here. in Spanish Honduras, sail blow off, and we had to beach the boat, to save the life of the crew.

The next one, she spring a leak, couldn't keep her afloat, and she sink down, but she never went to the bottom because we had in at least about 60 empty drum. We got in lifeboat and came ashore. She drift down a place they call . . . went there and salvage her.

Fishining at cays, would take 12 to 14 boats, two men in each. At Quita Suena no land at all, one little sandbar about a mile from the lighthouse, but can't live on it, too small, anchor the boat and fish . . . but Seranas have SW Cay, we call it South Cay, but the right name is SW Cay—that have 12 acres of land. Then you have Triangle, then you have Anchor Cay, then North Cay. At Roncador is only one cay . . . guana . . . plenty still there, manure. Would go every 15 or 20 days, bring in whatever the fishermen have, carry to market. Hawksbill run from 35-150 pounds. Also Green and Loggerhead, for meat only. Not around this island, on the Panamanian coast Green Turtle run up to 500 pound.

Big sharks? Seen them from boat, but not while fishing, around about 50-60 feet. I was on the MARY B, she was a boat around 45 ton, and I was laying down in the cabin and I feel like she was running on something, and when I come up I ask the mate what is the boat catching on . . . and when I look over the two fin was over the rail . . . head was nearly up to the bow . . . tail was about, at least as far as that little tree there astern of the boat . . . boat was more than 50 feet overall. Not a whale. I know a whale. I see several whales. The cobler on the bock, after it sink down and float bock, the cobler was about ten feet high off the bock! Black. Have square on it. No, I used to catch plenty of shark, skin them and sell the hide . . . for shoes . . . so you can't fool me with shark. In Caymans and all those island people catch plenty shark, the ile, put it in drum, sell it. Some say for lubricating airoplane or something like that.

For me the happiest time is right now. I don't got a job, spend time with my family. Well, in 1931-32 was when I had the most luck, able to work, go around, build this house. I can never say I had hard time, I always liked to work. But now I'm a little overweight and it give me pain in the knee.

Airport will be good, people should hold onto land . . . "

I thanked Capt. Eloseo for this opportunity to share his fascinating life, and walked on down the road with my tape recorder, daydreaming of those wonderful ships he sailed on . . .

CAPT. ELISANDRO ARCHBOLD JAN. 21, 1967

My grandfather was Ephream Archbold, then my father, Frederick, born on this island. He was captain of the RESTRAITE, government mailboat. He was washed overboard in 1942 on way to Cartegena and drowned. We were small kids. I was just about ready then to go to the continent to school. He was to take me back in Feb., and he drowned the 15th of January. Then I had to help myself. Morgan was the eldest, I was second. Home was in Smoothwater Bay. So we all had to help for ourself. So I went out from the time I was about 14 with my uncle, and then on sailing boat from here to Colon. Sometime I was sailor. Sometime I was cook. In 1920 when I was 17 I went on motor vessel from Canal Zone to Jamaica, Trinidad, up to New Orleans, loaded up and back to Honduras, then returned to Colon on another ship.

Fifteen days later signed up on a sailing ship, 2-masted schooner, the ARLY WILKSON. We take a load of rice and go into Norfolk, Virginia. I got off there. That was 1922. I went to New Orleans and caught a ship of the Standard Fruit Company, name of MARISA, running there about two years carrying bananas into New Orleans, no?

I leave off that one, went to the next one by name of YEARNY, to Honduras till 1925, then the DANELLA, a new ship, just come out, went to Colon, Jamaica, take fruit to New York. I made three trips on her, then sign on the American Dollar Line, 21 months. We cross the Pacific and back. I went to Philippine Islands, Hawaiian Islands,

Tacoma, San Francisco, and back to New York. Get paid off. Sign on then for another 21 month trip, 1928.

I went to Florida, was engaged then so went back to Florida and marry her. Then 15 days after I was marry I caught a ship back to New Orleans, took a Standard Fruit Company ship run to Vera Cruz, Mexico until 1932. I went back to stay with my wife, and never went back to sea then, stayed and worked in Florida six years till 1936 I leave from there and come home to the island, away for 16 years without coming back, my wife and four kids stay with my mother for around 8 months, leave and went down to Freshwater Bay and stay with my brother 10 months, bought a house here.

In 1938 I went to Cartegena and was mate on a 3-masted schooner, till end of '39. During war went to Colon, worked for Army and Navy for five years, boat captain, picked up several survivors, till termination of war. Came back here and built me a little house.

Leave from here and went to Santa Marta, was captain of ARRINA, in '46-'47. Bought a boat, was captain of her till '49, run from Santa Marts, take cattle to Curacao, Aruba, Barbados, Port of Spain. Returned home and bought a boat between me and my brother, small boat, 30 ton, the MARY DWELL. He was captain of her. In '54 that boat was bombed, sunk in the gulf of Cartegena. No, I was not on board. I was captain of the REMBREAU, for James Rankin. She was 69 feet, just the hull, without the bowsprit. I was captain of her till '52. Then I leave him and went with a boat by name of DELIVERANCE, till '54. I came home and went to the cays and fish, did fairly well. Fished for turtle as a boy also. I know every cay, Colombian cays and all the Nicaraguan coast, and also the Honduran coast.

Big sharks? I never saw one around the cays, but saw one in the Gulf of Cartegena. It was longer than the Rembreau. I tell you, it came right up under the boat, no? He come right up and knock the boat. His head was right under the bowsprit and tail was on the after end of the stern! And he push his two fins and come right up and latch the boat. The fin come right abreast of the full rigging. The tail didn't stick very high because she was under the bottom of the boat. Had spots, big spots all them size. I take the axe to chop the fin, but another man, an older man than me say no don't do it because he might whack and break something. Stayed there about 20 minutes . . . it was calm, no? Early in the morning, very little wind. Then after the wind start to come in, and the boat start moving, then gradually sinking until he disappear down. (Could it have been a whale?) No. It was a shark. After I steer off from him, he come up astern. The cobbler knife (dorsal fin), the cobbler, no? . . . come out of the water as high as that house . . . if you saw it in the sea you would think it was a sail, coming right up behind us. (about 10,12 feet?) Around 15, 20 feet. It was not a pretty sight. (so you think it was more than 70 feet long?) Yes, more than 70 feet. Because he was longer than the boat. The boat was 69 feet, And the tail was extend beyond the stern.

(Morgan Bush also saw a giant shark. When I asked how big it was, he replied: "Mr. Sid! it was longer than my boat . . . I didn't hang around to measure it!" These were undoubtedly Whale Sharks, known to be over 60 feet. Google will bring you much interesting information. Maybe you will discover why they seem to like to hang out under boats, in contact for many minutes—part of their mating behavior?)

Yes, then I take a sloop, yawl-rig, from San Andres by the name of PORCHIKA, and sail her from 1956 until 1960. She went down with me. Coming from Cartegena she sprung a leak in the night around 2:15 and around 4 o'clock ten of us on board had to start dumping cargo, to try to save the hull. We leave about 25 cases of cola and 4-5 cases of biscuits. I sail her under small sail until Wednesday, at 4 o'clock I was 57 miles off from San Andres I got into SE Cay 10 in the night, and she lose control, more than half full of water, pitch right back . . . and we turn her head to the SW, and I could neither get her head back nor up. I keep the two head sail on her and we come down till we pass south of SE Cay and near San Andres, about 4 o'clock I saw San Andres light, but then I was about 15 to 20 miles sou'west of the island, and it was blowing too hard and squally rough for me to take any chances in the lifeboat. One of the men says he saw the light. Well, I fool him, tell him no, that's a ship. If I didn't tell them so then it would be 9 men against one, they would want to take the lifeboat and pull back for the island . . . and there all of us would loose our life. The boat wasn't big enough.

Well, so I drift then . . . and that evening, four o'clock, I take a sight and I was 37 miles out from Corn Island. The boat head sou'west, but the current was sweeping to the nor'west, out from Corn Island . . . and we made this island called Lion Cay, south of Mosquito Cays, around 70 miles from Corn Island. 2 O'clock Friday night the boat went down, sunk. We didn't see the island, but we knew it was close. The boys told me: Capt. we can't hold her anymore. They were pumping and bailing right through, nobody take no rest. They threw the bucket right down on the deck and say: We can't go no more. So we throw the lifeboat overboard. I stood on deck and see that the nine of them get in the boat. I saw there was space for me, and I pass them two case of cola, take it out the box and stow it in the boat bottom. I guess it was six tin of biscuit, a couple of tins of milk, sardine, corned beef. I took off the compass, chronometer and sextant, a chart, parallel rule and divider, and put them all in the boat, and a can of water. So at five, five minutes to five, the boat sink. So I pulled astern of the boat about 20 feet, hold on with a rope about 20 minutes, then she went down and I cut loose. Bubbles started coming up . . . and I watched the bubbles till right out of sight.

Then we started steering by the compass and pulling on the oar, steering sou'west. And around 6:30 we saw Lyon Cay. We get there ten o'clock, pull up the boat . . . and saw where some people were there the day before. No one live on that cay. So we tie the boat good, and we all went to sleep . . . because five days we didn't have no rest. That was Saturday morning. At one o'clock I woke up and called them up. We had some corn beef and biscuit, and took a blanket and made a sail. We sail down about seven mile to another cay to the south of us, see where some was there in the morning, but no one was there. Another cay was to the SE of us, and when I look over there I see a sail stick up on the beach. So I continue to that cay again, there was two Nicaraguan, half Mosquito half Creole. They would get a bigger boat and take me to Corn Island, so they did. I sent a radio from Corn Island telling that the boat was lost, no? Then we get a pass on a small boat load with lumber and bananas.

I took sick and went to Baranquilla hospital, told me I had ulcerated stomach and gall stone, took an operation, cost me 30,800 pesos. I came back, and I give up the sea and become a farmer. Started raising cattle since 1963 and now I have 59 head. Had only a few acres, now I'm owner of 57 and a half acres, usually one head of cattle to an acre of grass. Just grass, no other feed, Guinea grass and Savannah grass. Savannah is better.

(how many people have more than 10 head of cattle?)
Alisandro Archbold 59
Capt. Ulric 40-odd
Woodrow 40
Cayatana Newball 100
Auntie Maude 10
Philipe Bryan 40
Victor Newball 20-odd
Alston Newball 10-odd
Elijah Bryan 20
James Rankin 20-odd
Rankin brothers 20-odd
Ronald Taylor
Wancho several more
Two thirds of homes have cow.
Six or more people on west side have over 10 each.
Antonio Bryan, my brother, have about 15, I believe.
Practically every house in Old Town have cow, 2,3,10.

I have one son who is the Captain Roosevelt, on Rosa Eugenia, and second engineer on the boat is Rudolpho, and Luto, Carlos, is in Bogota in school. Lisandro is a sailor on a schooner from San Andres to Cartegena, and two of my daughters are working in San Andres, one is married here in Freshwater Bay. The youngest of all, Marta, is in Chicago.

(is it true there are more islanders in US than here?)

No, I believe there are more born here who are away, but not in the States alone. You will find 800-900 in San Andres, a lot in Barranquilla, Cartegena, Bogota, Colon . . . mostly the highly educated are in Bogota.

(things in the night)

I never did see them. That is just imagination. I walked this island road right around from when I was a kid and I never did see nothing yet. You might have a little drink, you alone walking, and the wind blowing, and you see a tree moving . . . so I'm suspecting that's imagination.

Started building cement house, six rooms, plan to rent it.

(sadly, my tape ran out . . . thank you for sharing your life, Capt. Elisandro!

CAPTAIN SHERIDAN "SHERRY" ARCHBOLD

"I born in 1879. House in Bailey (which he rented to us in 1965) was father's and mother's home, we were born there. Father was Ishmael Archbold.

My first school days was at Kalalloo Point, I was living then in Rocky Point, the same spot where the house is, and we walk from there to Kalalloo Point, close to where Mr. Reed house is, just this side of the gully towards the point. Cousin Daniel was teaching school, Cousin Daniel Newball. I got up to 6th grade there, then after I was married in 1900, the mission asked me to teach school, but I must come to Panama, and I went over there and they give me the 7th grade, between Panama and Colon, and I come back here and taught school quite awhile in Rocky Point, you know where the Adventist church is? Well, I taught school there in that schoolhouse against it for the next two years. Then I went back and took the 8th grade.

Brother Rudolph used to teach there also. He became Adventist since we. We were the first Adventists on the island. My wife then had a young baby, Jenny, born 1905, the third child. We were both Baptists before that. My father was deacon. I think the Baptists go back to their parents. Four of us became Adventists. I attended the meetings every night, and I accepted it when the call was made.

Father Strobell, the Catholic priest, I remember him well. He was trying to make me a Catholic. No Catholics on Providence before, not attall. All Baptists, two Baptist church then, two brothers but they split, and one named Eusabia Howard went down close where the Catholic church is now . . . Eusabia was Ray Howard's father's uncle . . . his father was the one who remain in town. So I was a Baptist under him, under Ray's grandfather, until we accepted the Adventist faith.

Oh yes, I raise all my children as a sailor going to sea, and then I become a captain and learn navigation and I sail several vessels. I got upset in one. The first was a little boat for a lady in San Andres, then another one, the third I got upset coming up here from San Andres. My uncle was cook, he was below, drowned . . . he never got out. We drifted in two canoes . . . for 5 days and 6 nights. We drifted into Limon, 7 of us in the canoes, no food, not a thing for that period of time. We had some water, one of the boys that was on deck took it off, but it was raining all the time we were at sea. Shiver with the cold! But we live it out, without food, and we never drank water either, because never thirsty. Ship went right down . . . she was empty, belong to San Andres, see? to a man by name of Martinez, a rich fellow, have plenty of property, so he bought and give her to me to sell . . . but she got upset before she was paid for, so I never did own anything in her. Yes, then after that I start to teach school and taught till just a few years ago, for many years, over 20 years.

I guess times past were better for the people because they were more healthy, plenty food, labor was cheap, food was cheap. Had more farms, not so much people either. Flour, rice, sugar, corn used to come from the States by sailing ships, Bradley and his brothers, they always come here, bring cloth and all different things. Well, then they buy a load of coconuts back to the States. Flour in barrels. Things was cheap, very cheap. Money was better, on a par with American money, had plenty of everything. The people work more, produce better . . . now it's kind of like an old garment. All the earth, the richness is run off.

I would advise young people to work . . . (quietly) not to live here . . . live somewhere else. We have 11 children and only 3 is here right now . . . in the States we have one in Miami, one in New York, one in Washington, one in Panama, one in New Mexico, one in San Andres, one in Venezuella . . . marry there. Three ministers among our children, and three graduate nurses, graduate in United States and another graduate in Jamaica, from an American school.

We have several grandchildren! "Several" means quite a few! We never lost a child, my wife never miscarry. My father had 13 children, my mother 13. I don't know if there's any other. My mother is a Robinson before she marry. (Mrs. A. "I was a Robinson too.") Yes, my wife's parents, her father especially, was descended from white people who came here and got married here, Berelski . . . I think they got shipwrecked here. Then he changed his name to Robinson . . . so they are really Berelski, I think they came from Poland.

Elder Knight, Elder Goodrich . . . they were working down in Roatan and they built a sailing schooner and the mission sent them over here to make converts, from Belize and Roatan, and he sold books . . . and he pulled teeth, I think he was a dentist. Then afterward a doctor came, Dr. Echols, a very good doctor, established in San Andres first, got converts there and came back here the second time, then we accepted a few years later.

(Sadly, the next week on Jan. 22, 1967, Mrs. Archbold fell in bathroom and broke her hip, sailed on Arcabra (can you imagine the pain?), and on to a hospital on the continent. Capt. Sherry told me this when I saw him in San Andres on Feb. 9th.)

Thank you, Captain Sherry, for renting us your house in Bailey, and for sharing your wonderful life story!

CAPTAIN BALDWIN BRITTON

I was born in 1896, 20th of Nov. Well, my father died many years ago in Rocky Point. He tell me he have to work for himself from he was a boy, because his father die and his mother couldn't afford it. He raise the hog, and sold the hog to pay his schooling.

I had a very good brain, I could study very good, and there was a Jamaica man here, Mr. Reed, man and lady, a white woman, and they were staying down there where Frank and Jo Reed are staying now. There was a shop there and they give up the shop and are keeping school. Coming to school one morning with other boys (had been horsing around) and as them get to the door Mr. Reed had a big leather strap and whop him over the back! I says, "Mr. Reed, you're not going to whop me today. He says, "I will whop everyone that come in." And as I step in and he meant to whop me, I hold it, and I drag it away from him! . . . and I take my book and walk out, from that day until this day I never been back to school. All my schooling is in traveling. But in figuring, he told my father that he couldn't show me any more in figuring.

At that time my mother die, and my father marry again. Well, I went out and I come up till I was 18, and then I was trying to run away. I went down to the beach, had a little pig, had some clothes, and push off a little canoe down there was going to carry me to town. But an old Captain Hawkins came along and asked me, Son, where are you going? I was ashame now, and I waited till night and I carry my pack home.

Then that same old man they call Richard Taylor? Well, he was a young man and he came and was going to Bocas on a yawl boat by the name of the JESSIE NELL, and he send me along with him. I worked in a hospital, had a friend, Nick, boy about 15. One day at 12 somebody call him, and found he was not here. Well, after I came out from the kitchen, serving the patients, I asked for him. They said he is in the ward. Well, next morning, 7 o'clock, I ox for him again, because he and I supposed to be on the job. They said you will find him on #7 ward. Well, when I get up there I see the four corner of the sheet together and a safety pin in, and there was him pin up in there—dead! Well, knowledge shall increase as in the last days, and so it is. You know what the doctor did? He gave orders to put an ice bag on his head, and clotted those bloods. 8 o'clock he says, Britton, take another guy with you and take him down to the morgue. I was ignorant of the fact. I didn't know what was a morgue. But anyhow I stayed behind, and put the fellow before me ahead. Went down, and there was a table covered over with tin, and a big hole like that where the blood would run out, go down through a pipe and out to the sea. Doctor come down with mitten on, everything all covered up, big cigar in his mouth, first thing he did cut him from here come right up, put in big bottle with alcohol, and says, Allen, Britton, sew him up. My dear sir, to get a thin needle through this . . . sew him up . . . finish . . . and that was all I know of him. I never see him anymore . . .

From there I left, went to Almirante with this same Richard Taylor, send me to work on the dock on the ship, load bananas. Big white fellow there . . . first time I going to work. I was young, young boy, don't know anything, 18 years . . . and I look down the ship hold and all I see was smoke . . . they had on the freezer now, to take on the bananas. I put my head down, sniffed, went up in the nostril like that, and I wouldn't go. So when he come, he curse at me! God-damm-it now, I told you to get down in the hold! I told the time keeper I was going home. I went downstairs, and I left . . . I gone and I got a job on the dredge.

Well, they put us to chop down grass, big Guinea grass, high now, about 50 of us, but I'm afraid of snake . . . all of them gone! My dear Mr. Sid, when I look like from here to the door there was one coiled high as that, thick as that! And about this much of him going like that, licking his tongue! And I fling the machete, I don't know where it is until this day, and I run.

And after I get to the beach where the dredge was pumping the sand, I see one of the pontoon gone like that, and a fellow gone down in the sea. I swim to the pontoon and I put him on. His name was Cushman, a young Jamaican guy. Well, I went aboard and asked them to give me my time, but they said not before the last of the month. I says OK, I walk and catch the launch for Bocas, the CRESTAN, and I went up and took a schooner DELMA to Colon. And that was the night they had a great big fire, mon! And I had fever. I hold my belly and I vomit. I went down to the beach, and everybody by the hundred, by the thousand, laying down there sleeping the night. The American government went out by the commissary and blow up a whole block of houses from Cristobal, from the Canal Zone right across, to stop the fire. Couldn't stop it. That was 1915.

So I was working in the Canal on a tugboat by the name of PARANILLA. I was a dayman, cleaning the brass. We had an old captain name of Richard Frost, big old man, and he make me a sailor. I work 38 months and 20 days to the day I land back here and I was 21 years old, and from then I looking for myself.

Well, every cent that I earn I know where it goes to, I had a little book and I check it. If I trim hair, I check it. If I buy a piece of chance, I check it there. I wanted to know what I'm working for. The old man wrote me and tell me he's going to build a boat, he use the money that I sent home. I wrote back and tell him no, I don't like a vessel, I like a business. When I came home, Andres O'Neil along here, Mr. Bowie from San Andres and him, three of them, built her right down there where you see that little coconut grove, south of where you was staying there . . . there where she was built . . . her name was PHILADELPHIA, 38 tons, she was a yawl. I remember the day we went to pick ballast in her, those black rocks, heavy, smooth, from down Black Bay.

And from then, I been around the United States for years, had a whole lot of discharge. I came to one, I was getting $52.53 a month, so I get a discharge from her. I went down to pier 13, saw a big black policeman, said would you allow me to go aboard that ship? He says sure, go ahead. So I went aboard and ask for a job. The Ist Asst says, can you fire? I says, no sir, I'm a sailor. Well, he says go down below and tell junior . . . I didn't know what was a junior. I went down and there was an old guy. I says is it you who is junior down here? He say, yes. I said the 1st Asst sent me down to learn how to fire. He said, all right. And we leave that same night to Chile. And the third night we leave out of there I was in charge of 12 fires. Big ship, bring ore from Chile to Baltimore. I made a couple of trips on her. I didn't like it.

Once we were going to dock up there, the mate says Britton, it's snowing tonight. I didn't know what was snow. When we went up on deck you would slide . . . I was dropping right on the deck.

After, I went to jine the IWW . . . Industrial Workers of the World? the union, paid for six month, payman was after me almost everyday (laugh). Well, I been all around, going from boat to boat. Quit one of them and went to a boarding house there, didn't like the way they going, drink too much, too much noise, so I went down below. A guy come, ask where you from. I says I'm from Providence. He says I'm Haitian, didn't know you were from Providence, RI. But I didn't say any more, didn't tell him I'm from Old Providence Island. Two policemen came in and went to the counter. The guy used to make corn whiskey underneath the counter. They took him off, and gone.

About the same time I went to a Spanish boarding house. My dear
Mr. Sid, it was cold, February month. The second day skipper called
me, asked if I want to ship out. I said yes. I tell you I was running
with that ship until I had trouble getting off her. They didn't want
me to leave. Finally, I leave and come home.

Well, been all around. Been on one for United Fruit Company,
used to leave from Curacau, Honduras, Bocas, Almirante, Christobal.
When we was going into Port Limon the mate comes to us, says, well
boys, all of the wages will be cut. But I'm asking you all one thing,
don't you quit. Well, we was now going to Mobile, Alabama. He says
to me, Britton, the ship will be haul up now, I don't know for how
long, but I don't want you to leave. You will get nothing but your food.
Nobody will be aboard but you two, I said, no, I have to go. I go with
a big Caymanian fellow on Greyhound bus to New Orleans.

A policeman was coming up, heaving his stick, says where are you
guys going? I says a car is picking us up taking us to the dockyard. He
says, OK. Shipping commissioner shipped us all out . . . for 1 cent
a month! At sea mate came around, said Britton, you going to work
today. I said no, not me, I didn't come as a working man. I ship out as
a sailor for 1 cent a month to go to Christobal, the company put me
back there. I wouldn't work. We pass Cuba, Rosaland Bank . . . come
to Queena . . . then I know we are nearing home . . . my dear Mr. Sid,
that day when we pass Old Providence in the month of March, and
I look and see the men chopping down cane . . . I says to the mate
will you come closer to the white water and let me swim ashore? He
says, oh no! Next day we was in Christobal. The mate said you are all
coming here as workmen, but he said to me, take a taxi and get away,
I'm giving you the chance. So I took a taxi right away.

After that I ship all around, but I can't leave home for long, and
all that you see here these two hands given by the blessing of God,
work by my machete. I had orange trees, Leslie, Elibur, Rayford,
Winslow. I cut down the orange trees and plant coconut. Yes, all the
boys gone, couldn't handle it.

Leslie is here, lives right down there, first cement house on the
right. Elibur is captain of a boat. Leslie is an engineer. Rayford is in
Lincoln, Nebraska, leaving this month for Dearborn, Michigan to

work for Ford, married to a Baranquilla girl has been studying all the while, got his degree now, $830 a month starting him at, and all facilities, everything free.

And this one (pointing to picture on wall), he is in Mexico, a dentist. Six years he study in Mexico. I spent 17,00 pesos to get his visa, been after it three years, just get it now. He came home on vacation 2 years ago and when he went back he was wanting it and make him trouble. They are very strict over there. He says that in 7 years he will be a millionaire. Plenty of money when it's American money you work for. So he put up his own office now.

I had a daughter, she was married in Bogota, she died now. I have a daughter in the US now, but they don't know the mother. She is studying and working in the hospital, yes sir, staying with an Adventist family over there. And this one I'm taking up tomorrow night with me to go to Medellin.

Built store in Rocky Point in 1955.

(forgot to tell me of being Captain of the RESOLUTE. Conversation rambled . . . salvaging lumber from wrecks, one sank far offshore but lumber drifted in. Stories of James Rankin, Bob Marx, "Bandit", buying and losing land, mistakes made in building airport and road.)

(Before leaving I took picture of Capt. Baldwin and Miss Bernie in front of their house).

Thank you for sharing your amazing experiences around the world, and the exciting future of your children!

MISS BRES

Mrs. Bresilda Viude de Gomez, affectionately known as "Miss Bres", as island nurse, has been an intimate friend to virtually every family on Old Providence Island, delivering babies, giving shots, even making ice cream (for many years, the only ice cream on the island.)

I remember one night, Dec. 30, 1966, my wife and I were coming back in the pickup after exploring Bat Hole at Southwest Bay, when we stopped and waited outside a house where Miss Bress was delivering a baby.

Children were peeking in the door while the father paced around the yard. Four little girls were running around, when finally came the new baby's loud, strong cry! Then a voice from the window, "It's a boy!" Boys in pick-up were chattering about their girl friends, but hard to follow as it started pouring rain. We were still waiting for Miss Bres. Finally, she came running, and my wife, Ali, shared the front seat with her back to town.

On Feb. 3, 1967 I had the pleasure of tape-recording Miss Bres as she told me the story of her life:

"Yes, I was born here. My mother is one Camelia Taylor, and my father Franklin Carpus. Lived in Old Town. No, there were no nurses at that time. From the island here there have been quite a few, but they go away to study and they don't come back. Well, before I came back home, because I made my studies in Cartegena, there was a nurse, a Spanish nurse here, but before they just used to use midwives that

135

from one generation to another they hand down what they knew, but not trained nurse.

I born here, but my mother used to live in Corn Island. I had two friends down there that were nurses, no? one Filia Welton and one Casilda Morgan, so from a little girl I always had it in mind that I would want to become a nurse. Well, after my mother died I gave up the idea of becoming a nurse, so I was in Cartegena and was reading a book and I come across an address said if you want to become a nurse to write to the Chicago School of Nursing, and I did send the coupon, and they started sending me tracts and so on, and I got interested, so I started to take that course. Then afterward I went to the hospital and university in Cartegena and continued there, but I still owe most of the little that I do know, which is not much, to the Chicago School of Nursing.

I am 48 now, and 21 from 48 . . . came back to the island at 27.

(Tell me what you did today)

Well, I went to Southwest Bay and I applied 25 vaccine, no? for smallpox, for all ages. And from 7 years to a year I injected 15 vaccinations, we call it the triplet, no?—that is against Diphtheria, Whooping Cough, and Tetanus. And then I applied 30 doses of anti-tetanic vaccine in adults. That has to be 3 doses, from 3-5 months to have the second, and then in three months the last one, no? About 10% of islanders have had tetanus shots. You know, the people at the beginning you just couldn't get them to do, but then when a case of it come up you tell them they can be protected . . . and little by little . . . (Did Alvaro Garcia have tetanus?)

He developed tetanus! He was here and some of the people said it was useless for him to go to San Andres, but I told them that if he stayed here he would die, but if he went to San Andres he would stand a chance, because we didn't have the drugs here to treat him, and sure enough by the time he got to San Andres he was worse because he had stoppage of water and all . . . he was at the Sanidad here and said: my jaw is getting stiff, so I said you must go to the doctor at once because you are developing Tetanus, I'm sure. Well, we are always handicapped here, no transportation, our service too limited, and even for the work we do two nurses is not sufficient.

(are there still midwives of the old fashioned kind?)

Yes, two . . . I do most of the deliveries . . . island mothers have very easy labor compared to other places. Once, maybe in 50 or 100 cases there might be a little complication, no? but most of them are always just a normal birth.

I can think of about 25 mothers that have had more than ten children, but I know there are others I have not attended. One has had 17 children, all alive. More than half of island mothers nurse their babies."

When I was visiting Providence in 1999 I talked with Miss Bres as she was playing dominoes with a friend in the evening, and thanked her for her wonderful ice cream. She said she is still making it!

Miss Bres, on behalf of all the thousands of islanders who you have helped over the years we want to try feebly to express our very deep gratitude to you. We love you!

JULIUS BRYAN

(taped life story 1/12/67)

"Julius Bryan, the same one!

99 on 16th of Dec. . . . the eldest one (on Providence)(laughing)

Born right in this same Bottom House . . . you American mon, no? Go to Mobile but I never go to NY. Yes, a sailing boat.

When I was a boy used to pick cotton, and they had a gin where they ginning it, no? They had a cocos stick . . . ? . . . bales of 300 pounds. . . . cotton, shit! When we get to Mobile, the vessel anchor, the next day the cotton higher than this house.

(a little boy, Heiro?, took hold of my shirt and touched my arm)

He call me grandfather, you know . . . a pile of them . . . a whole pile of them! How many? No, I can't count because I have some Colon too.

I born 1868, be soon 100, mon. I (will) live over 100 you know!

In the olden day mon live to 500 year, ja.

When my grandfather was old, rode horse . . . one wreck up Rocador name BUCKINGHAM . . . shit, the bottles were full, all over the sand. Oh, mon! Plenty liquor! The richest wreck was ARGWAN, Ronc ador, everything in thot! All everything most that you can call for!

This is my daughter, you know. How many grandchildren? You would have to take a foolscap paper and when you write it full, and turn it, and write it full again! Aunt Ella alone have 15, Catherine have 10 or 11, your mother have 11. Auntie Ersula have 4, . . . have about 10 . . . I can't remember how many! . . . Ensela have 4, and I have 2, Uncle John have 3 . . . I couldn't name them . . . because it's a great amount! And he has more great grandchildren than what he has grandchildren. And there are children, you know, live in Colon.

(A great family!) Well, you see, when I was young, I never drink rum. A dentist from San Andres come, take out all teeth.

Sailed on several vessel, several mon . . . Fred Robinson, had several . . . died over 30 years ago . . . Fred was a farmer.

(interrupted by child falling down)

The same woman there call me grandfather, you know?

Ray Howard don't take another woman yet?

(I promised to come back for his 100th birthday)

MISS ZEPPORAH BRITTON

When I visited "Aunti Bora" on Jan. 9, 1967 she was 90, baby chicks under the house clearly audible on my tape recorder.

"Most old pictures lost . . . plenty hurricane, they spoil.

My father was Lemuel Newball, lived in Smoothwater Bay. Mother was from Rocky Point, just before you get to Capt., two boys still in the house. build over.

Uncle Daniel Newball was teacher, at Kallaloo Point, Alston Newball's father . . . one of the daughter still live in the house.

Father Strobelle was one of the first priests come here, then Father John, Father James . . . and the next one, not remember all.

No Catholics at all on the island before Farther Strobelle, none attall . . . only Baptists and Adventists.

Island more prosperous when she was a girl, things cheaper . . . 5 pesos for flour, now it's 135-40. We wasn't as wise as now, you see, but things were cheaper. Capt. Knighton and Capt. Wilbank and Capt. Fred . . . them come from the States and bring things cheap, big ships come to buy cotton.

Used to work it right around the island, and they had a gin, bag it up . . . people used to go aboard then and buy what they want, corned beef and all those things.

Born in 1877, no slave was done away with, no more slave. Each family worked their own cotton, and they help each other gin it, no? Everybody used to work the cotton. Plenty cow, used to sell it to San

Andres, same as now. Ships came by town, never around the east side. A little cotton still grown for sale to Cartegena up to World War II.

Have ten children . . . Timothy in Bogota, a civil engineer . . . Dyonesio in Baltimore, a psychiatrist . . . Rubin in Colon (picture on wall . . . one son dead . . . a daughter in Cartegena, Sarah Archbold . . . and my mother die too . . . one sick, Alberto Britton . . . one in Panama, Zepporah . . . one in Old Town, Almina Britton . . . two dead . . . and I raise six other children, Oswaldo (outside) I raise him from seven years. One boy of 19 drowned.

I've come to the age where I'm not coming or going (laughing to lady visitor) You still look good, Miss Bora!

I feel all right.

(baby chicks still peeping under house!)

Thank you, Miss Bora for giving us first hand memories of Providence life . . . in the late 1800's! . . . truly remarkable!

CONCH AQUACULTURE

Before divers learned to use flippers and masks, it was much more difficult to harvest conchs, but for many years the Queen Conch has been over-harvested, conch chowder and fritters becoming more and more expensive. This is very sad—for the conch, for us, and our grandchildren.

By the 1970's conchs were no longer harvestable in Florida, and had to be imported from the Bahamas and Caribbean.

Now there is an exciting, but expensive, ray of hope—conch aquaculture. At Harbor Branch Oceanographic they have recently learned how to allow female conchs to lay egg masses in captivity, so it is no longer necessary to search for wild sources of eggs. They hope soon to grow conchs "from egg to entree"—though of course it will take at least seven years before we can have our first farmed conch chowder.

Other saleable products (in addition to the shells themselves), are jewelry, horns, and conch pearls, to name a few.

At Key West there is now a "Conch Baby Farm" where visitors can see how the Mote Marine Laboratory grows baby conchs for release in the wild. At the same lab coral fragments from damaged reefs are taken to new locations and firmly attached so they can continue growing.

Problems with conch aquaculture include predators (crabs, fish, lobsters) which eat the juveniles. Sadly, these farmed juveniles do not learn to burrow in the sand for safety as they do in the wild.

Maybe some of you in Providence can learn from these successes and failures to plan something even better for the future of the Queen Conch.

Google: conch baby farm
          Breakthrough event in queen conch aquaculture
          Harbor branch aquaculture
          Conch predators

NATURE'S AQUARIUM-TERRARIUM IN THE TREES

Bromeliad's are one of Nature's most amazing ecosystems. Their giant leaves (something like a pineapple) making a fence a foot or so in diameter which then captures a pool of rainwater. Gradually a whole community of creatures begin to spend part of their life here: mosquitoes and frogs lay their eggs: larvae and tadpoles soon grow into mosquitoes and baby frogs, high in the trees! But that is just the bare beginning. There are snakes, lizards, mice, humming birds, butterflies, crabs, snails, spiders, and insects of many kinds. Startlingly, scientists have found over 300 other species in bromeliads, both plants and animals.

Ants of several species even protect the bromeliad by attacking intruding insects. Biologists are only just beginning to study this world of creatures in the tropical forest canopy where nearly half of Earth's species live. We haven't mentioned the microscopic life. It is truly a thriving "zoo" high in the trees.

Life in bromeliads is so varied that it creates its own fertilizer and soil. Many species here never touch the ground. Some poison dart frogs are found only here.

If you are a science teacher in Providence or other tropical area, and you can find a bromeliad low enough for safe climbing, you might put it in a large tub or other container and study it. while much of its community of life continues as you watch. Of course you will warn your students never to touch a poison dart frog. With magnifying glasses and low powered dissecting microscopes, you can make a long list of your own fascinating discoveries.

Afterwards, maybe you can even return it to its original spot.

Some bromeliads are up to three feet in diameter. I think you will be content with a much smaller one!

In the Science Times section of the June 16, 1992 issue of The New York Times, is one of the best articles ever written about bromeliads: "Natural Terrariums Of the Forest Canopy."

PLANKTON

Plankton, drifting in our planet's oceans, are more important for all life than most people realize. Drifting with the currents, they may be divided into three groups.

Phytoplankton are microscopic plants with chlorophyll, able to make their own food through photosynthesis—one of the basic miracles of life on earth. Along with bacteria they are the base of our planet's food chain. Two small for us to see with our naked eye, they are present by the thousands in every bucket of sea water, as a microscope at 100x magnification will show you.

Zooplankton are microscopic animals. The microscope will reveal them too, the ones that are moving, swimming! We have talked elsewhere about Euglena, which have green chlorophyll—but also swim! So scientists had to create a third kingdom for them, Protista—creatures which have characteristics of both plants and animals.

Macrozooplankton are those big enough to see with the naked eye, but still small enough that a cup of seawater will contain thousands. They will include fish eggs and larvae, and invertebrates—creatures without backbones. A microscope at lower magnification will reveal them—a truly remarkable world of beautiful creatures no human artist could have invented.

You may enjoy the challenge of trying to draw them in color as you watch. One of your drawings could become a birthday card for someone you love. They will be so grateful to share in your "adventure in marine biology".

For more fascinating information about this miniature world, Google: plankton.

IGUANA FARMING

Sadly, the Green Iguana is on the endangered list. Once plentiful throughout the Americas and Caribbean, because they are so tasty to eat and easy to catch, they have suffered severely from over hunting. Once living in the trees of almost every yard, they are now seldom seen.

The good news is that iguana farming is now successful in Costa Rica and an increasing number of places. But won't poaching destroy these farms? Interestingly, not so. Farming brings the price down and the eyes of the whole community are watching, encouraging success. Why bother to catch an iguana secretly, when you can buy one at the market for about the price of a chicken?

An area with plenty of large trees will not require expensive cages. Iguanas tend to stay in the forrested area. If their numbers increase to the point that they are crowded and tend to go looking for another territory, great! The farm is succeeding.

For more detailed information, Google: Iguana farming

POISONOUS & VENOMOUS

A tropical island, even the most beautiful in the Caribbean, and the coral reefs surrounding it, are not without their dangers. We have already mentioned Cockspur and Manchioneal, shrubs and trees to be carefully avoided.

At any tropical beach, when wading in the shallows, it is wise to slide your feet slowly along the bottom, rather than walking rapidly or running, so as to chase away any sting ray which might jab you with the stinger on its tail.

"Fire coral" or "stinging coral" (Millepora) though not a true coral, is very common, growing on dead coral or rocks. Whitish or yellowish, it is easy to learn to recognize. Of course you should never touch any corals, because they are easily broken, take years to grow, and can cause you to suffer a sleepless night.

The Portuguese Man-of-war is the most dangerous creature to swimmers and divers. With a purple inflated float it "sails" in the wind and current along the surface, dangling long streamers of stinging cells below it, sometimes extending six feet or much more. Like thousands of swimmers, I have lost a night's sleep several times merely be touching a few tentacles wound around an anchor rope, stepping on some washed up on the beach, or contacting a small one in the sea. Many swimmers are taken to the hospital for such minor contacts. Vinegar will help, but who carries vinegar? Pee on it!

But this creature can be far more dangerous than these minor contacts. I'll tell you of two personal friends, who both say they could have died.

On Jan. 24, 1966 my friend Alvaro Garcia had full contact with a large Portuguese Man-of-war across his chest and shoulder, some around onto back, arms and legs. Alvaro is one of the most skilled and experienced divers I know, not afraid of sharks. He was spearing fish with friends, watching a nearby shark, when he came up under it. Pain was immediate, and disabling. Friends had to lift him into boat and carry him to Dr. Conolly who gave him an injection. Frank Reed saw him being carried screaming past Alcalde's office. His friend Mariano said he was "out of his mind".

I saw him at 3 PM, still in severe pain, writhing and groaning. I came back the next day. He had a bad sleepless night . . . "raving" . . . but was now resting peacefully, quite rational. I took two photos. His buddy suffered many stings also, just in pulling off tentacles.

My friend Bob Straughan was collecting aquarium fish alone in Biscayne Bay, Miami, Florida, when he also came up under a large Man-of-war. The pain was so disabling that he might have drowned if he hadn't been rescued by a passing boat. At first they thought he was a madman, were hesitant to approach because of his screaming. He also has life-long scars.

Rather than list other hazards I recommend you buy the Peterson Field Guide, Coral Reefs, Caribbean and Florida.

DEADLY BOX JELLYFISH

Recently at Australia's Great Barrier Reef, and then around the world, several species of tiny jellyfish have proven to be deadly, probably responsible for over a hundred deaths in recent years, whose causes at the time were unknown. They have even been found seasonally in the Caribbean. Sadly, this is important enough that all swimmers and divers should become informed.

We recommend that all swimmers, divers, and boat operators carry a bottle of vinegar with you in your dive bag, for immediate use on all stings of unknown origin.

Some are so tiny, and hard to see, that it took scientists many days to catch one—even though they were searching purposely and full time. But if you go to Australia please be prepared. Wear a lycra full body suit, and mask. Sadly, you should not expect the authorities to educate and warn you, as some of them are so interested in tourist dollars that they may not wish to scare you off.

In the Caribbean you may be safe for now (except for the Portuguese Man of War), but keep informed.

Google: Box Jellyfish, and Venomous Sea Creatures.

In Providence the responsibility will fall on dive instructors and science teachers to keep all islanders and visitors well informed.

One major article is: KILLERS IN PARADISE, The Tropics Are Home to the World's Most Venomous Creatures—Jellyfish With 4 Brains, 24 Eyes and Stingers that Can Kill You in a Minute Flat, by Paul Raffaele, Smithsonian, June, 2005

SEAWHIP ADVENTURES
WITH UPJOHN

One day in 1970 I got a phone call that changed my life. It was from Dr. John Pike, a research scientist at the Upjohn Company, a large pharmaceutical firm in Kalamazoo, Michigan. He had read of my Adventures in Marine Biology at Old Providence Island, where there were many seawhips. They were researching a new medicine called prostaglandins, and had just discovered that the exact compounds they needed were present in a soft coral seawhip called Plexaura homomalla—could I get some for them? He sent me an article, which mentioned that one of the products which could be made from prostaglandins might be a once-a-month birth control. I was deeply concerned about world population explosion, and believed that couples should be able to plan their children by choice. No one wants abortion. It was family planning by choice that I was in favor of, so I told Upjohn I would like to come to Kalamazoo at my own expense to discuss how I might become involved. They said for me to please come at their expense.

So, four wonderful years with Upjohn began—collecting specimens all over the Caribbean from Bahamas to Turks & Caicos to find out where the right kinds of seawhips grew, doing a regrowth test at Grand Cayman Islands—taking photos each month of harvested colonies . . . then harvesting in the Bahamas for four years.

I built a harvesting raft, worked with a Bahamian diver, Curtis, who picked up what I cut—and his uncle who chopped and packed on the raft. Full boxes went to the freezing plant. At end of week we loaded my truck, which just filled a twin-engined Beechcraft to Miami, where I saw it off to Upjohn, and I went home for a week with Ali and the kids. So it went . . . for four amazing years . . . I commuted from Connecticut to the Bahamas . . . getting paid for what I love most . . . diving!

Finally Upjohn learned to synthesize prostaglandins, so the project was over. Ali was able to join me occasionally for a few days of snorkeling in the Bahamas, but it was wonderful to be home with the kids again, and to start going back together to Old Providence Island!

OUR MARINE BIOLOGISTS

My members in Adventures in Marine Biology and I were so fortunate that such a wonderful group of marine biologists agreed to become our teachers.

The first was Dr. Victor G. Springer, Ichthyologist, who was eager to make a large collection of Bahamian reef fish . . . In daily classes he taught us the basics of fish anatomy, and encouraged us to be careful observers as we helped him collect.

Dr. Eugenie Clark came next. After reading her books it was exciting to snorkel with her on the reefs, and learn of her newest research.

Dr. John Storr was interesting in a quieter way. His lectures were overpowered by seeing whales and having a minor wreck.

Bob Straughan, though not a marine biologist, was utterly fascinating because of his thousands of hours experience underwater, and his ability to catch fascinating specimens every day to watch in aquariums—basket starfish, swimming scallops.

Dr. Jim Tyler taught us a wide variety of insights as we watched him do his own special research, catching fish which live inside of sponges. He dissected a shark on the beach with our group and many islanders watching (including the mayor and science teacher.) (see photo on cover) Alejandro (Alex) Landano Garcia, a marine biology graduate student from Bogota, was our guest, later holding a high position in Colombia.

Dr. Marston Bates was my biggest mistake. Intrigued by his interesting books, I was not aware that he couldn't snorkel and was an alcoholic. A nice person, but . . . very sad.

Dr. Carter Gilbert, ichthyologist from Univ. of Florida taught us how similar fish on opposite sides of isthmus of Panama had evolved with slight differences since the time when the oceans were connected. Also, a similar evolution in small lakes which were once connected.

Dr. Lou Disalvo was contagious in his love of marine biology. A guest was Jorn Geister, at that time a graduate student at University of Bern, Switzerland, later to become a world expert on coral reefs, writing the definitive papers on San Andres and Providencia.

And last was Ben Rose, of the Underwater Explorers Club, Grand Bahama. Like Bob Straughan, though not a marine biologist, he had thousands of hours experience in the sea, had made a special study of gobies. He kept us all fascinated by hundreds of interesting observations, and photographed the new Hamlet, first seen at Providence.

The following are a few scientific papers published by our leaders from their research at Providence:

Louis H. DiSalvo, REGENERATIVE FUNCTIONS AND MICROBIAL ECOLOGY OF CORAL REEFS: LABELED BACTERIA IN A CORAL REEF MICROCOSM, Biol. Ecol., 1971.

James C. Tyler and James E. Bohlke, RECORDS OF SPONGE-DWELLING FISHES, PRIMARILY OF THE CARIBBEAN, Bulletin of Marine Science, Sept. 1972.

Jorn Geister, Bern (after many papers, this is his major monograph), Modern Reef Development and Cenozoic Evolution of an Oceanic Island Reef Complex: Isla de Providencia (Western Caribbean Sea, Colombia).

I'm sure there are others I don't know about.

PHOTOS

In addition to the photos on the cover and inside this book, there are also 300 more photos available to you on CD or DVD, in 3 groups (most from color slides):

Group A—our first trip to Providence in 1965, and island life at that time.

Group B—our visits 1968-72, islanders interviewed, and Adventures in Marine Biology groups.

Group C—my experiences working with the Upjohn Company (major pharmaceutical manufacturer), when they were making medicines (prostaglandins) from seawhips (soft corals), including survey trips around Caribbean, regrowth studies at Grand Cayman, and harvesting at Andros, Bahamas.

You can order them from me, view them on TV, print those you want on your color printer. If you wish to publish any of them, I would appreciate knowing your plans, and will give permission, possibly asking a fee.

If you take photos related to marine biology or Providence, please send them, maybe to be printed in next edition.

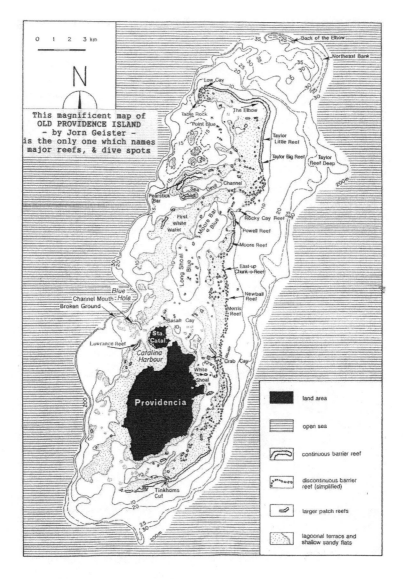

Map of Old Providence Island by Dr. Jorn Geister

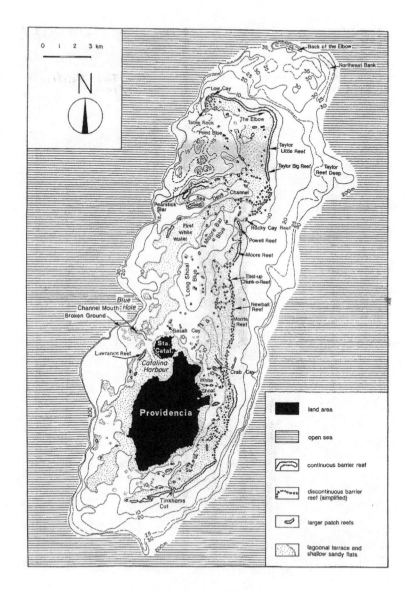

Map of Providencia with place names

Our house in Bailey 1965 rented from Capt. "Sherry"

Neighbor's hen laying egg in our chair

Neighbor showing iguanas to Ali and Bryn

Craig, Ali, Bryn on horseback 1968

Author holding Portuguese Man of War

Dr. Jim Taylor explaining specimens to members of
Adventures in Marine Biology, August, 1959

Ali and Bryn with unusually beautiful Queen Conch

Ali with bread, fresh-baked over charcoal 1965

Cat boat racing

Ali with inflatable kayak and raft, collecting shells

Capt. Ulric Archbold going ashore from Arcabra

Oscar

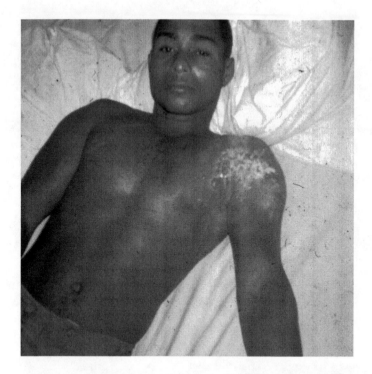

Alvaro Garcia day after hit by Portuguese Man of War

"Cockspur" (*Acacia collinsii*)

Cat boat with sail folded, conchs, island fisherman

Shark (just caught) on our raft August 1968

Raft designed and built by author, with member-divers

Dr. Jim Tyler dissecting shark, Alejandro Londono Garcia
(guest from the University of Bogota), members, and islanders

Air view, sea whip collecting area. Grand Cayman Island

Motor Vessel "Arcabra", loading cattle & oranges

Our son Craig diving with Ali (before he was born!)

Author with octopus

Author below large Elkhorn Coral (photo by Ali)

PLEXAURA HOMOMALLA   before harvesting

The sea whip, *Plexaura homomalla*, before harvesting

Regrowth photo, to document recovery after harvesting

Diver holding background-board for regrowth study photos

first written '67 Noroton, CT
Free Verse

FRIEND OF THE DOLPHIN

Reefs of Nature's Childhood—a Salty Dream

The Sea is my second home . . .
I am a friend of the dolphin . . .

I snorkel along the edge of the reef,
The sun warming, browning my back . . .
Two barracuda . . . slow, following me . . .
All of their teeth in good order.

I dive . . . down-coasting . . . slowly . . .
Towards the green-blue coral . . .
The Grouper, from his cave, peers out . . .
Long, at each other, we gaze quietly . . .
I turn . . . slow-floating towards the sun.

I see the fisherman up above,
Looking down through his glass-bottomed bucket . . .
A sad-friendly grin of envy . . . he can't swim . . .
All day with hand line he fishes . . . and may catch nothing.

Look! The Hogfish, far below, head-standing down in the coral . . .
I dive, spear close by my side . . .
Coasting slowly, no move by hands or flippers . . .
Sideways he turns now to view me . . .
What stranger now coming? . . . no teeth? . . . no . . . moving so slowly.
Hogfish don't know, but it's me, now coming for dinner.
Slow turning . . . to look with his right eye—spear fly!
Hogfish tastes good for our dinner!

Yes, the Sea is my second home . . .
I am a friend of the dolphin . . .

"I wish I could do thot!" . . . fisherman, from boat calling,
"Aren't you afraid of the sharks?"

Yes . . . he's big fish, but . . . not too brave.
Circling, he stays far out . . . careful . . . to watch me.
Most always I've time first to see him . . .
But if I first come close, before he sees me . . .
Then that old shark is scared . . . not me!
I see only his tail fin . . . going far through the coral.

But, when I spear fish for dinner,
Old shark . . . I don't trust him.
From far down the reef he can feel . . . hear the fish-cry . . .
Fish-cry is sad . . . but, for shark, it's dinner bell . . .
Fast he now comes swimming wild in!
First thing his eye catch is hurt fish . . . he think,
But it's me! He rush me fast now—not lazy-scared like before.
Now, with dinner bell ringing, shark comes fast in . . .
Like fin-tailed torpedo!
Till, almost here, he sees I'm not fish—stop! wrong way!
Fish-cry down there—fast he turn . . .
Shake fish like dog with meat too big to swallow.
Careful now, I swim sad back to boat . . .
Shark got our dinner.
Yes . . . the shark . . . sometimes I do fear him.

Goodbye now to fisherman . . .
The reef is waiting . . . my thoughts turn to the 'morrow . . .

The green-blue Sea is my second home . . .
I am a friend of the dolphin . . .

For you, friend fisherman, or your brother on the shore,
It may seem strange, hard to believe,
But 'tomorrow' my flippered mate and I, with our children,
Will call from the shallows to our dolphin friends,
And there they will come . . . slowly at first . . . but then
With joyful cries to answer our shouts and laughter.
Together will we cavort the hours away in the emerald foam,
Each shouting joy in his own language . . .
But . . . for those who see beneath-the-surface . . .
There need be no interpreter.

Holding to their great fins *
We will follow . . . on their carefree wanderings . . .
Where beauty and adventure wait . . .

Then, with arms about their broad necks, *
We will swim together through the reefs of Nature's Childhood . . .

Nature's childhood . . . yes
For we seek Something there . . . Something we have lost . . .

We Men, oft unknowing, yearn to regain
Our brotherhood with all Animals . . .
Imagine an antelope with lumbago . . . a dolphin with ulcers . . .
A jaguar wearing glasses . . . an otter dying of heart-attack . . .
Or even a raccoon with a bad cold . . . can you?

---

* Thoughts of putting our arms around dolphins came before we snorkeled with Dr. Denise Herzing, Wild Dolphin Project, learning to befriend dolphins . . . only "in their world, on their terms."

Only the Sea, now, is left
Where Man can venture into pre-history,
Can see and participate with Nature . . . untouched,
Can explore, like primeval savages,
Wonders no human eye has seen.
There can we marvel at Evolution . . . in progress . . .
How did the Sargassum Fish get that way?
Looking almost like the Sargassum Weed . . .
And, as we gaze and ponder . . . and new insights come . . .
How did Man get that way? . . . how the 'great gap' . . .
Seemingly . . . between us and other animals?
How did Man become intelligent? And then . . .
Yes, we must ask it . . . how did Man become . . . neurotic?
Imagine a deer sadistic to its fawns,
Seals having slaves, or tribal wars . . . can you?
Could it be true, as it seems, that the only neurotic animals
Are humans . . . and those domesticated by us?

In the Sea, Man finds deep, almost unknowable, longings . . .
To recapture childhood Joys . . .
To feel our body . . . warm . . . comfortable . . . whole . . .
To glide, soar, dive, wheel, and hover . . .
To gaze at beauty in unselfconscious wonder . . .
To see real dangers face to face . . . and survive unhurt . . .

Man, the hunter-gatherer . . .
Bringing home fresh food . . . still wet with salt . . .
A far cry from the supermarket . . . a far cry from the office.

In the fishing village where children play . . . naked-brown . . .
Warm in the sun and foam . . . sharing friendship and love—
In varying degree—with every man, child, dog, baby, woman . . .
Including their own parents . . . but with everyone . . . a far cry.

As we marvel, in the Sea, and later ponder by the fire . . . alone
And together . . . How can civilized Man regain what he has lost
Without losing what he has gained?
Is that too much to ask?
Many say yes . . . far too much . . .
And not to be desired anyway . . . but . . . sadly . . .
Look at us . . . and our children . . . often afraid of the water . . .
Never having played naked in the Sun . . .
Terrified by joyous movement . . . cringing from blood . . . or sex . . .
Even avoiding the warm gaze of another's eyes . . .
Growing into mothers who shun breast feeding . . .
Fathers who cannot cry . . . and therefore cannot be soft . . .
Afraid of the dark . . .
Hating school . . . lost—the joy of learning . . .
Of self-reliance . . . self-discipline . . .
Too often suffering . . . sadness . . . loneliness . . .

We turn to the Sea not only for fun, food, health . . .
But seeking new insights . . . even a new way of life . . .

At dusk, my flippered mate and I, with our children,
Will return to the sands . . . to sleep 'neath a tree-shaded roof,
With friends to share music . . . dancing . . . learning . . . work . . .
For on the 'morrow we till the field
And perform other duties . . . creative and routine . . .
But we will return . . . to play again . . . in the Sea . . .

For the Sea is our second home . . .
We are friends of the dolphin.

(added . . . 9/19/2000)

How fortunate are the children of the fishing villages of Earth!
To swim . . . ride . . . sing . . . dance . . . play . . . love . . .
Welcomed in many homes . . .
Sitting in the sand . . . in awe . . . as an elder tells a story
Helping an aunt, cooking at sunrise . . . smoky aromas . . .
Rewarded by a delicacy . . . the taste lingeringly delicious . . .
Watching an uncle make a net . . . holding the threads . . .
Being needed . . . as a helper . . .
Running . . . down the beach with friends . . . the wind in our
hair . . .
Gathering and eating fruit, ripe from the tree
Sent on an errand by mother . . . a smile and a hug on returning

Father's boat is coming in . . . we run into the surf to help . . .
Carry a basket of Red Snapper to shade of coconut trees,
Watch grandma sharpen her knife and filet the fish,
Yearning to try it someday . . .
Carry some fish home to mother, and neighbor . . .
Run to collect freshly laid eggs . . . real taste . . . no hormones . . .

Swim with friends . . . wish I could dive like him . . . I'll learn!
Drifting weightless in sparkling sunlit white-sand shallows . . .
Lying in warm grass . . . to marvel at the sky . . .
Cloud patterns stirring dreams of imagination . . .
Marveling at halos around leaves and creatures . . .
Brilliant flying specks . . . randomly curving . . . in the blue . . .

How fortunate are the children
Of the fishing villages of Earth!
Seashores, rivers, lakes . . . Caribbean . . . Polynesia . . .

Learning to weave, to throw a net . . . being needed . . .
Hungry! heading home at sunset for a plate of steaming food . . .
Joining village families around a fire
To sing . . . and dance . . . Listen to an elder's story . . .
Gazing up, with Wonder . . . at the glory of the stars . . .

The joys of the extended family
So often now lost to children of Earth's cities . . .
More crowded by the moment . . .
Doubling again before our children are grown . . .

How fortunate are the children
Of the fishing villages of Earth!

The sea is their second home
They are friends of the dolphin . . .

END

This salty dream . . . is for Ali . . . with love . . . remembering the many
leagues we snorkeled . . . together . . . sometimes with dolphins!

INTERESTING EVENTS AT PROVIDENCE

1527—The "Universal Chart" shows unnamed island.

1629—Christmas day, two ships land with Puritan colonists.

1631—Seaflower brings more settlers.

1636—(Providence, Rhode Island founded by Roger Williams.)

1640—Pimienta captures Providence, deports Puritans.

1640-60—Island is Spanish prison.

1666—Captured by Mansfield and Morgan.

1670—("New" Providence Island (Bahamas) founded by Eng.)

1670—Taken by Henry Morgan on way to sack of Panama.

1688—Spain reports "no inhabitants"—a century "unknown".

1776—(Unites Stated Independence.)

1787—Given to Spain by Treaty of Versailles.

1789—Francis Archbold given land grant by Spain.

1794—(French Revolution.)

1795—O'Neill becomes Governor.

1806—(Captain Bligh "takes possession" at San Andres.)

1808—Ceded to Province of New Grenada.

1810—Governor O'Neill retires.

1815—(Napoleon defeated at Waterloo.)

1817-21—Commodore Luis Aury makes island his headquarters.

1822—Providence becomes part of Colombia.

1849—(California "gold rush"—steamships to Panama)

1853—Slavery abolished in Providence.

1861-65—(Civil War in US.)

1903—(Panama Canal opens.)

1904—(Wright brothers' first flight.)

1920-37—(Prohibition in US, stills on Providence.)

1931—Prosperity peaks, plague hits crops, economy declines.

1938—US President Franklin D. Roosevelt visits.

1953—(Air service begins at San Andres)

1956—(San Andres becomes "Free Port".)

1967—Air strip opens, Aeroislena first air service from SA.

2000—Declared UNESCO "SEAFLOWER Biosphere Reserve".

2007—This book published, 300 photos available on CD & DVD.

SOME COMMENTS ABOUT JANE PORTER'S "NARRATIVE"

SIR EDWARD SEAWARD'S NARRATIVE OF HIS SHIPWRECK, AND CONSEQUENT DISCOVERY OF CERTAIN ISLANDS IN THE CARIBBEAN SEA: WITH A DETAIL OF MANY EXTRAORDINARY AND HIGHLY INTERESTING EVENTS IN HIS LIFE, FROM THE YEAR 1733 TO 1749, AS WRITTEN IN HIS OWN DIARY. EDITED BY MISS JANE PORTER, IN THREE VOLUMES. London, 1831.

I have the 1834 edition, and read it with great interest, but gradually became a skeptic. It's a good story, but now I'm quite sure it's fiction. Others feel the same way, though many stubbornly wish to think it's true. But, at Old Providence Island, there are no lobsters with giant claws as in New England, and never have been. Many other things described in his "narrative" could never have been found at Providence.

Jane Porter, who called herself the "editor", was a prolific writer at the time. Shipwrecks and wonderful fantasies were popular over many years, into the present: Robinson Crusoe, Swiss Family Robinson, Treasure Island, Moby Dick, and many others.

Miss Porter's book was so popular she was able to have it published in many editions, beginning in 1831. Now a fairly rare book, it is fairly difficult to find and expensive to buy.

Even though fantasy, maybe some movie producer will come to Providence and film a big hit, "on location". They certainly could with Morgan and Aury. They are just waiting for someone—maybe you—to write the film script!

A CHALLENGE TO A PROVIDENCE DIVER

Sadly, many islanders have never personally seen the underwater wonders which surround them. You could help. You could teach some friends to snorkel. You could get or make a few aquariums for schools and public places, catch beautiful creatures for all to enjoy. (Plate glass can be glued together with a tube of clear silicone rubber from a hardware store.) Some hand nets, air pump, and instruction book will soon build your experience. Start with only two or three creatures. Otherwise overpopulation might kill them all.

One creature, easily caught but seldom seen, is the seahorse. You can find then clinging to grass in the shallows off Southwest Bay, and probably many other places.

Another amazing creature is the basket star fish. They are most active at night, their many arms catching tiny plankton creatures drifting in the current. They are seldom seen by divers, because in the daytime their habitats of waving soft corals don't seem interesting. Go to a shallow patch not far from town on the way to Lawrence Reef. Look very carefully and you will find them, their finger-like arms up to two feet long. Pick a small one with arms about one foot long and break off a bit of rock or coral that it is attached to. (You will need a hammer and small crow bar.) Put it in an aquarium by itself.

Then you might like to go to the dock at night with a bright light. All sorts of tiny creatures will come to the light. There will be plankton forms of many larger fish and sea creatures. With a fine mesh plankton net you can scoop them up and add them to your basket starfish aquarium—and watch what happens!

When scuba diving over a sandy bottom, you may disturb some scallops, which will "swim" away, flapping their shells. You won't believe it till you see it! Catch a few (quite a challenge!) Then, in an aquarium, your friends can see them swimming, and at last believe you. Google: Calico scallop, Smithsonian

On shallow reefs you can catch gorgeous fish. Try for the smallest, and only two or three. At first, while you are learning, it might be best to let them go again after a few days. When you become an expert you may learn to keep them for months or years, even rear a second generation of young.

Put in some snails to clean algae off the glass. Also two hermit crabs will be very entertaining, especially if you also put in four empty shells so you can watch them try out a new home. If they don't like the fit of the new one, they will quickly jump back into the old.

Catch one very small crab (not a hermit crab) which will choose a corner and try to catch small fish as they pass. A cowry shell (which you can find under large rocks) will be a beautiful sight as it slowly roams around.

One or two snapping shrimp or coral shrimp are as beautiful as they are hard to catch. The tiniest minnows you can catch will be tasty food for them and the larger fish. Some fish may be vegetarians, so you will need some algae (which will give off oxygen for the fish, and take in their waste carbon dioxide. Your aquarium is becoming "balanced", like our blue green planet Earth. You might get four small limpets (which you can find on smooth rocks) one to crawl around on each pane of glass.

Get a copy of THE SALT-WATER AQUARIUM IN THE HOME by Robert Straughan, from Amazon,com. There are many more recent books, but his is excellent. If you can't get it, write me and I will send you mine, autographed by the author in 1959.

You might like to wade or snorkel though the shallows around the mangroves. This is the nursery for many species. Once when I waded there near the airport to gather oysters to eat, I was bitten on the finger by a ten-inch long moray eel, the only time I ever saw a small one. He would be king of an aquarium!

Another time, nearby, snorkeling in two feet of water, I watched an eight-inch barracuda for several minutes. These babies are seldom seen, but would be great to watch. There are an unlimited number of small fish and other creatures for your aquariums. Rather than trying to make big sweeps with your hand net, you will find it more effective to hold the net still and chase the fish in with your other hand.

You will have an exciting time and will enrich the lives of your fellow islanders. Work with the science teachers, who will be happy to make educational signs.

You might help organize a group of volunteers (maybe a school science class) who would like to reintroduce turtle eggs to beaches such as Mona bay, hoping that when the hatchlings grow up they will return here to lay their eggs. This may have been done already as a Seaflower project, but there would be no harm in doing it again. The Archie Carr group could help you obtain eggs, and provide advice.

We would not like to encourage anyone to collect anything from the sea—for sale. There are better ways to make a living. Sadly, collecting black coral and other creatures can be very dangerous (divers have gotten the bends, even died)—and it is very unhealthy for the future of our reefs.

You can easily help prevent damage to the reefs by some simple education. Tourists and inexperienced snorkelers do not know that coral is a living creature—which takes many years to grow. They should learn never to stand on coral, or even touch it. Encourage them to be proud of learning these simple skills. Stand only on sand. Never hold onto coral. Besides damaging a wonderfully beautiful creature which took years to grow, you will also damage yourself, suffering sleepless nights with terrible itching and burning.

You can make some simple signs at boat docks, and wherever swimmers and snorkelers enter the water. You could even print a small leaflet to be given to tourists arriving by boat or plane.

Let me know your experiences, problems and successes—your own adventures in marine biology. My very best wishes to you!

BECOMING AN AMATEUR NATURALIST

What is an "amateur naturalist"? I like to think it is anyone who enjoys carefully observing Nature, and learning from the wonders which surround us everywhere, everyday. We can help children have these adventures from a very early age.

For instance, a spider on its web is certainly one of the wonders of NATURE, which can be found close by, anywhere. To help a child catch an insect, throw it into the web, and watch what happens—can be a memorable experience. Then watching the spider spin a new web becomes even more fascinating.

There were a series of such experiences which brought excitement and wonder to me, and changed my life. "If my words did glow with the gold of sunshine"*, I could share them with you, and change your life, but my feeble words are probably not adequate. Maybe you would need to "be there" with me, at age ten, on a north China beach, to scramble at low tide over the seaweed and starfish covered rocks as the sun rises—to marvel at the tide pools, brimming with sea anemones in rainbow colors, their tentacles waving, ready to grasp any passing creature.

Coming to a flat ledge dropping into deeper water, the temptation was irresistible to kneel, eyes in the water, to see "beneath-the-surface". It was a blur, but . . . there was a fish!

An article in AMERICAN BOY MAGAZINE had instructions for carving goggles out of balsa wood. After a week of work, mine were finally ready. They didn't fit perfectly but well enough to give a few seconds of clear vision beneath the surface before they filled with water. I was hooked! My love of the Sea grew through a lifetime.

In 1933, my dad took me to the World's Fair in Chicago, "A Century of Progress". I was eleven. The free exhibits were the most interesting. I was intrigued by the "color organ", projecting on a curved screen a different color for each note, a rainbow for a cord, a moving rainbow for music.

But nearby were three huge screens which captivated me far more, microscope projections of living creatures! . . . paramecium, amoeba, euglena . . . I didn't know their names yet, but knew they were alive, and swimming in a drop of water! I came back night after night for the whole week, told my parents I wanted a microscope. I didn't know it yet, but already I was an amateur naturalist.

I read Rachel Carson, Archie Carr, and so many others.

I joined the Norwalk skin diving club, learned to snorkel, spear fish, scuba dive—even won two trophies for best spearfisherman.

I made a huge saltwater aquarium in our home. We watched crabs planting seaweed on their own backs, starfish moving towards food, hermit crabs trying a new shell. It was better than television!

My wife, Ali, and I paddled kayaks with Orcas off Vancouver Island, swam with sea lions in the Galapagos Islands (in Darwin's footsteps), snorkeled with wild dolphins with Denise Herzing's Wild Dolphin Project in the Bahamas, were thrilled on television by Richard Attenborough's LIFE ON EARTH.

The tireless skill of nature photographers reveal the lives of wild creatures (as if we are there to see for ourselves!) how they raise their young with consistent discipline and firsthand experience . . . so that they learn to take care of themselves (probably more efficiently than most humans)—with no crime, no psychosis, little illness. Do these problems come only with "domestication" . . . which interferes with the basic natural functions of Nature?

Old Providence Island, and most every island on Earth, now have satellite dishes, so Nature programs are available to all. Darwin would have marveled at the wonders revealed by their close-up photography!

An amazing example is the Madagascar orchid with nectar tube over eleven inches long. Both Darwin and Wallace, knowing that orchids are pollinated by moths, independently predicted that there was an unknown nocturnal moth with tongue that long. Recently a nature photographer proved them right with photos of a new species of moth pollinating this orchid! And that's not the end. An American entomologist, Gene Kritsky, has found another Madagascar orchid with even deeper "rostrellum". He hopes "that we won't have to wait 41 years before this new predicted moth will be found." Institut Virtuel de Cryptozoologie predicted moth.

Since an island is the world in miniature, we are all "islanders". So, islander, no matter where you live or how you make a living—you can also be an amateur naturalist. Wake each morning to marvel at this wondrous Universe of which we are a living part! Enjoy practicing careful observation. Each hour will bring you new wonders. For instance, watching birds feed outside our window, a pair of Cardinals which usually eat separately (he even chasing her away) . . . suddenly, one day in spring, there he is feeding her, beak-to-beak! I wrote it down in my diary, and then, the next spring, we saw them again!

Throughout each day, as you go about your daily chores, you will see bits of Nature you never noticed before. Even more exciting, you can help the children in your life become amateur naturalists also. It will change your life, and theirs!

It's my most sincere wish that more and more "islanders" will become amateur naturalists—especially you!

Some very highly recommended books:

THE AMATEUR NATURALIST, by Gerald Durrell
PETERSON FIELD GUIDES, by Eugene H. Kaplan
Coral Reefs, Caribbean and Florida
Southeastern and Caribbean Seashores

THE VOYAGE OF THE BEAGLE, by the youthful
Charles Darwin
THE SEA TURTLE—So Excellente a Fishe, by Archie Carr

Please take me seriously! These are books you will want to own,
read more than once, loan to friends. Buy them second hand on ebay,
all at once . . . they will be shipped free.
Google: Dr. Archie Carr, A Tribute & Marine Turtles, NOAA
If you are thinking seriously about a job, you can check out:
Careers, Jobs in Marine Biology & Oceanography, by J. Wible.

IS PROVIDENCE FOR YOU?

Many maps of the Caribbean do not even show Old Providence Island. It has no jets, no cruise ships, no large hotels.

If you are looking for nightclubs, casinos, guided tours, fancy restaurants, luxury hotels—with service to make you feel like royalty—sorry, Old Providence is not for you.

Seeking easy drugs? You had better stay home . . . and change your lifestyle.

Want inexpensive, easy, totally safe travel—I'm afraid not, but where can you find that these days?

If you are a land-developer or hotel-builder, looking for an exciting investment opportunity—forget it. The islanders have everything in hand. This is their island.

What's left?

Well, if you like snorkeling and diving, horseback riding and hiking, small comfortable guest houses, real Caribbean island food—with no one trying to make you feel like royalty—then, it would be very sad for you to miss Old Providence Island. You will be welcomed—to Paradise!

If you are looking for possibly the most gorgeous coral reefs in the Caribbean, they are here! When Ben Rose came from the Underwater Explorers Society in Grand Bahama to be our leader in 1972, he admitted: "The Bahamas are very beautiful, but they can't match this!"

If you are a scientist, yes! Providence might be an ideal place for you, in most any field of research, most not yet explored.

If you are a nature-lover, this is not Costa Rica, but it would be hard to find a more beautiful island, so much to teach you. And Costa Rica is close, possibly with flights from San Andres, so you could go there too. We very highly recommend Costa Rica, the country which abolished its army to put all resources into education and national parks! Many Providence students have gone there to college.

If you are an active senior citizen looking for a most beautiful and healthy setting, you may not find many fellow senior tourists here, but you will love it, and can bring your friends next time.

If you are a world-traveling backpacker, you will find many fellow wanderers here. Read about Old Providence Island in LONELY PLANET and other travel guides. Yes, definitely! If you add Old Providence to your destinations, it could be your most memorable adventure.

So, Old Providence Island is not for everyone, but, for you, it just might be the most wonderful island you ever discovered. In 2000 it became the UNESCO Seaflower Biosphere Reserve, many feel the most beautiful spot in the Caribbean.

BON VOYAGE

Well . . . here we are, my friends . . . Islanders . . .
adventurers in marine biology
amateur naturalists
sailing on our wondrous blue-green planet Earth
in this miraculous Universe
sparkling with Energy
and love . . .

Bon Voyage !